"Success is not final, failure is not fatal:
it is the courage to continue that counts."

—Sir Winston Churchill

THE VENN
EFFECT

THE VENN EFFECT

An Entrepreneur's Guide to Success Through Purpose
Second Edition

W.K. (BILL) RADER

Isabella Media Inc

THE VENN EFFECT
An Isabella Media Book
Isabella Media E-book edition/October 2019
Isabella Media Hardback edition/October 2019
Copyright © 2018 Isabella Media Inc

Library of Congress Catalog Card Number: Pending

Website: www.isabellamedia.com
Author Website: www.billrader.com

Published simultaneously in the US and Canada
PRINTED IN THE UNITED STATES OF AMERICA
ISBN: 978-1-7330416-2-1

For my Father: My first editor, who taught me that nothing is more important than integrity.

For my Mother: My enabler and the one who believed in me before anyone else.

For my Wife: Who has stood by me through sunshine and storms.

CONTENTS

FOREWORD

by —Carl J. Yankowski

BILL RADER FIRST CONTACTED ME ON THE social media platform LinkedIn. He reached out with a message that caught my attention—he wanted my assistance in starting a venture that would help others. I used my network to do a check on Bill to learn more about him and his background. Once satisfied, I agreed to talk with him. Later, I would join his fledgling company, Efferent Labs. His vision for this company was one I latched onto eagerly.

As Bill and I worked together to build the initial foundation of Efferent Labs, we shared our stories and backgrounds and gained a deep mutual respect and friendship. Our discussions ranged widely based on our experiences over decades in the business world. While Bill is relating his personal story in the Venn Effect, this book is helpful to any business. Bill has applied his underlying principle in life to all his business ventures: "Do what you love. Do what you know."

This book is a rare look at common considerations made throughout Bill's career spanning five unique businesses.

Bill started his first business as a teenager. He gained success in a unique field by improving production processes, based on his own trial and error—the best way to learn. After selling his first company at the age of 18, he went on to serve his country as a nuclear engineer for the Navy, shipping out on ballistic missile submarines in the latter years of the Cold War.

When he left the Navy, Bill's inventive proclivities led him through a series of successful, and unsuccessful, start-up experiences which served to educate him, in business and in life.

By themselves, these lessons learned came at a time he needed them, and collectively provided Bill a firm foundation of discipline needed for success.

In the Venn Effect, Bill relates lifestyle as a critical element of entrepreneurism. This lesson was one that was taught to him through many life lessons on his journey, and then really driven home through a diagnosis of Multiple Sclerosis in 2009, and the challenges in the following years that a disease such as this presents.

His start-up, Efferent Labs, is a medical technology company built around implantable biosensors, designed to serve as a real-time monitoring system within the human body using the patient's own living cells. This can allow doctors and caregivers to "see" what is happening inside a person at a cellular level in real time.

Bill did not invent this device; he went looking for a technology to change the world after a rare connotation of his MS had paralyzed him from the neck down and left him in a wheelchair in 2011. His experiences with his brilliant doctors and caregivers, as well as the introspection brought on by an extended stay at the Mayo Clinic, caused him to want to create and build something that would improve the lives of patients.

The search for a world-changing product led Bill to the University of Rochester, School of Medicine and Dentistry, and Dr. Spencer Rosero. Dr. Rosero's team was the first in the nation to implant the St. Jude heart pod device to replace leaky cardiac valves. Spencer had invented the implantable device and was looking for someone to help develop it to full commercial viability.

Bill and Spencer found that they share the same passion and complement each other very well. They personally risked their own monies to get the company started. With their leadership, they ensure that Efferent Labs is an honest company which demonstrates measurable proof of design and functionality of the CytoComm™ device at every critical milestone.

Efferent means "conducted outward." The company has conducted itself outward with an unchanging focus on where we were in the developmental process. Intent, purpose, ideas, and plans are always crystal clear to stakeholders and stockholders. Due to the vast experience Bill has, and the added knowledge and expertise brought in by the industry experts on the team, Efferent Labs has always had clear, solid goals through every stage of the development process.

The team has had its challenges in starting Efferent Labs. The company was passed over by investors many times, yet they refused to give up and continued to network aggressively to find investors who understand the technology and the vision. The team always firmed up the same ideas. They expected the unexpected to shore up weaknesses. All team members spoke with one voice. They never oversold.

The Venn Effect describes Bill's journey from naïve teen to an embattled and experienced business veteran and provides a unique insight into how you may also come to find what you love to do.

Carl Yankowski
Chairman, The Westerham Group

Carl J. Yankowski is an internationally known and respected businessman. As the first four-time Fortune 500 President or CEO (Reebok, Palm, Cadbury-Schweppes and President & COO for Sony Electronics) he has served as Chairman or Director of numerous organizations including Chase Corporation, Novell Inc., Polaroid, CRF Health and many others. He is a graduate of the Massachusetts Institute of Technology and Wellesley College.

PREFACE

I WAS INVITED TO WRITE FOR *FORBES* MAGAZINE in the spring of 2016. The reason they asked about my interest in writing for their publication was simple: I had won the largest business competition in the world.

In October 2014, my company Efferent Labs, Inc. placed second in the inaugural 43North business competition, now held annually in Buffalo, New York.

But, even with their invitation, the *Forbes* editors were only asking if I was interested in applying to write for their periodical. They wanted to test my ability to provide the content they desired and to ensure it was good enough to be included in one of the world's most prestigious business publications. Lucky for me, this was not my first foray into the world of writing a magazine column.

My First Writing Gig

In the early 1990s, the chief editor of Triple-D Publishing's *Home Theater* magazine contacted me. The publication was predominantly focused on audio products and the then up-and-coming home theater marketplace. However, they were also interested in expanding into an area where I had expertise—home automation.

At this time, home automation was still considered something from the classic 1960s children's cartoon "The Jetsons"; cool but futuristic technology. Changing a television channel by remote control in the 1990s was standard, but operating one's home under conditional timing control (also known as automation) was virtually unheard of and considered something only the rich and famous could afford—which mostly, it was.

The editor contacted me because he needed someone to write a column about the fledgling consumer home automation market and other electronics of reader interest for his magazine.

Because I was naïve to what writing for a periodical was all about, I grabbed the opportunity and ran with it. I had recently founded the home automation company Hybrid Technical Systems, Inc. and looked at this as a great way to advertise my company.

I thought to myself, "How hard could this writing thing really be?" and jumped at the opportunity.

I approached the prospect knowing nothing about the periodical business or what it took to be a writer for a national magazine. To start, I had no—I mean zero—idea of the editorial process. I had never thought about this aspect of the job. I figured I would write about something and it would be published. No pressure. Easy-peasy. I was wrong.

Upon signing on the bottom line of Triple-D Publishing's very lengthy contract, I committed myself to write the stories, providing all photos and submitting each completed article to my editor for inclusion into the magazine on a firm schedule.

When I was invited to the first quarterly editorial meeting, I thought that I would listen, drink a soda, and nod occasionally. What happened was I was asked to pitch ideas for stories and then was nudged into doing what was required by the magazine to satisfy advertisers.

The worst part was that I had committed to complete my stories three full months prior to publishing. This meant that I was already behind.

The magazine had to sell advertising, lay out the issue—using the now old-fashioned method of storyboards hung on the office wall—and edit the content. This took time, and the editors wanted the stories available for layout on schedule. The process from start to finish was three months per article.

I walked away from my first editorial meeting with notes on what I needed to research and write about. But, also wondering how I would catch up and get ahead of my committed schedule.

This may sound easy, but it was not my full-time job, just a side gig that paid around $300 a month. I was not doing this for the money, but as a way to promote my company. It was essentially free advertising from my view. However, in reality, it was far from free. The time and effort required to produce a good story was obviously much greater than I had anticipated.

I enlisted the help of my father to be my first-pass editor because I did not want to turn in less-than-perfect work. Even more important, I knew at least a quarter-million subscribers were paying to read my articles, as well as a large number of newsstand readers. I wanted my articles to look good and have usable content.

My father turned out to be an excellent editor: timely and fantastic at catching items like misused metaphors and improperly structured sentences. I was grateful to have his help because without it, the editors would have shown me the door long before my first article hit the newsstand.

Often when one writes for a popular publication, offers arrive from other periodicals with similar needs. Writing for *Home Theater* magazine brought with it a request to write a couple of stories for *Electronic House* magazine.

Flash forward twenty years. The *Forbes* editor was requesting a similar column, one that covered a different subject area.

Forbes

With the *Forbes* opportunity came a repeat of my first writing gig. They didn't just take my word I could write for them. *Forbes* editors required I submit a writing sample and a bunch of story ideas to see if I could meet their needs. The interview and contracting process took a couple of months, with my first *Forbes* story being an introduction to who I am and why I had some authority to write for their publication. But more so, why people should read my stories. This time the audience was not a few hundred thousand, but potentially millions.

The editor asked me to provide insight as to why a reader should read my stories. He asked me to answer a question in my first column:

"What authority do I have to write about entrepreneurship and business?"

He was also the one who told me what the audience was looking for in my inaugural story. He said, "Think about it, Bill. Talk about where you came from and tell *your* story. It caught us, and if you write it, they will read and enjoy it."

I decided to go back to my beginnings and take a snapshot view of my "real" companies. I skipped over stories of selling plums and lawn mowing and went straight to the one I loved. The one that put me on my path to where I am today.

My first *Forbes* story was not an easy one to compose. Writing "30 Years, 5 Start-ups, 4 Exits: My Lifestyle" was a journey for me, captured in roughly one thousand words. It debuted in July 2016. This story was one of the hardest things I had written up to that time. I had to do a basic introspection on my life and put it on a platform where all the world could see it, comment on it, and critique it.

In this piece, I focused on lessons learned, keeping almost all company information and names to myself.

I turned this *Forbes* story into a keynote speech entitled *The Venn Effect: Lessons of a Life Long Entrepreneur*, one I have given many times since.

Forbes—July 2016
30 Years, 5 Start-ups, 4 Exits: My Lifestyle

Entrepreneurism is more than just a word to me—it's my lifestyle. In this, my inaugural column, I chronicle some lessons I have learned in my journey that have brought me to where I am now. In future columns, I will write about all things associated with being the CEO of a start-up.

As a lifelong entrepreneur, I have been down many roads. Many were difficult, but all were interesting.

Life as an entrepreneur can be both daunting and exhilarating. It's the chase, I suppose, that is so much fun for me; it's the results (most of the time) which are so rewarding. The rewards don't necessarily need to be monetary, but more the satisfaction of doing something new, better, or impactful.

My Journey

I sold my first business at age 18. I loved the business, the process, and the results. I started the business two-and-a-half years prior and made what was a decent living for an adult, while only a teenager. I discovered that a product was in great demand and engineered a process to supply a better product, in higher quantity, faster and more consistently than my competitors. At the time, I didn't even know the word "entrepreneur." However, I learned how to build a business under-fire and in the local library.

When I sold the business, I made money that would help fund my next venture several years later. It also paid for a really nice sports car.

I also received my first business lesson:

#1—Do what you love.

However, a young entrepreneur doesn't necessarily heed his own advice. In my next venture, I did not follow lesson number one, thus starting a journey to my great awakening. I spent a lot of time creating my idea and fleshing out all the details. This was the pre-Internet age. I had to do my researching in libraries, and although the idea seemed solid, I didn't really know the industry I was entering and had done nothing even close. I was a young hotshot who had sold his company a few years earlier and thought I knew everything.

Scratch that—when the rubber met the road, I really didn't know what I was doing, and I paid for it dearly. At the end of company number two, there was no sports car, savings or really anything other than a pile of trampled pride.

But I took away another lesson:

#2—Do what you know.

Brushing myself off after this pride-robbing venture, I briefly considered working a normal job. But, as a born entrepreneur, it's not in my DNA to work for the man. Soon, I found myself doing what I loved and loving what I knew—starting another business.

This company used my education, experience and personal passion. In business, timing is everything, and it was an early time in a young industry. We had a best-selling software product and the largest market footprint for our hardware products.

However, it was still a niche market that appealed mainly to hobbyists (code word for nerds). As I was building this company, I determined that my business had limitations because of the early stage of the market. When I was presented the opportunity to sell the company, I did. Although I loved what I was doing, I wanted to pursue something that had better growth potential.

Next Lesson:

#3—Timing is everything.

The next venture was more of a journey, and more than likely the longest time I would ever devote to a company. I founded Raland Technologies using all my lessons. I knew my business; the timing was right, and I was doing what I loved—the business trifecta. I spent the better part of the next two decades developing, building, and promoting the company—building it into an entity with locations in multiple states and operations internationally. I employed a multitude of people and experienced the difficulties of several economic cycles. Along the way, I encountered all the issues one can imagine: client, employee, legal, and government. I was able to experience the best of business and the worst, in equal glory.

During my nearly twenty years with this company, I also had many life changes: from the highs of getting married to the lows of receiving a horrible disease diagnosis.

My diagnosis of Multiple Sclerosis radically changed my life both personally and in business. A year after diagnosis, I found myself laid up in the Mayo Clinic, paralyzed. The illness hit me hard, and I was in the clinic for a couple months as the physicians worked diligently to get me back on my feet. You have a lot of time to think when you're lying in a hospital, unable to move.

Creating a company that was very successful is one thing, but the question that kept coming to me was, "have you made a real difference?" I could justify a "yes" by saying I employ scores of people and that my company does great things. It just was not the "yes" I needed.

Last Lesson:

#4—*Success is more than a dollar sign.*

This was my "Great Awakening," and I looked for my next venture in a wheelchair. I embarked on a trek across the United States and, in the end, was introduced to my new venture. I found what I was looking for, not in the halls of Johns Hopkins, where I had ventured in my pursuit, but in my backyard. Through networking, travel, talking, and listening, I found my calling in Rochester, NY.

The Result

I founded Efferent Labs, a biotechnology company, with a technology created by my co-founder Dr. Spencer Rosero of the University of Rochester. When I met Spencer, things clicked in a way that is needed to be successful. We had the experience, passion, and drive, and the time was perfect. His ideas had just become feasible due to technological advances. Together, we formed the nucleus of the team we are building—a team that has the vision, passion, ability, and drive to ensure our success.

Since our initial meeting a few short years ago, we have made scientific history by watching cellular activity live in vivo. In October 2014, we were a winner in 43North, the $5 million start-up competition, based out of Buffalo, NY. We also moved into offices at the University at Buffalo's Center for Bioinformatics and Life Sciences. We are advancing a product that will help millions of people. We have been awarded patents and started the large effort of pitching investors to help in moving our product forward to those in need. Life is short, but I have found that it is the journey that is the reward. In my articles, I will tell you my story—the story of a lifelong entrepreneur on a quest to build a company that will help people.

* * *

This story summarized the inspiration for all my activities today. It defined my experience and the motivation I had for starting my company, Efferent Labs. It outlines my seminal reasons for being and the direction I am heading.

It was amazing to me that I could capture so much in so few words. I don't know if readers came away with the same profound revelation as to my personal "why" because they never saw the how, when, and where. I revealed only a tiny peek into my motivation.

Writing can do this for a person: provide an outlet for exploration of desires and dreams. But, in my stories, I had another mission—mentoring. I felt the best way to give back to others was to provide insight into my thoughts as an entrepreneur, believing there must be a little educational value in my story for someone.

Evidently there was because within a year another major publication, *Inc. Magazine* approached me. They asked me to write the column *Leadership and Viewpoints* for their online platform. I did, but for a much shorter period of time.

There was a clear stylistic difference required by *Inc.* than how I enjoy writing. The biggest difference was the amount of content. I like to write complete stories, ones that require at least 800 words. *Inc.* asked me a couple of times to make the content I provided much shorter. I felt that my style would not be a good fit for them. Adding in the fact I had so many other duties running a company, I just didn't have any time to write for both *Inc.* and *Forbes* concurrently.

So, I contacted my *Inc.* editor and left the publication within six months, after only three published columns.

My experience writing the *Forbes* stories ended up providing a new goal. While writing my first column, I did a tremendous amount of introspection. Writing about my lessons learned reminded me of so many things I had done and of the great people with which I had done them. I started telling the stories to my wife and told her I would write about them in a book someday.

About a year after *Forbes* published my first story, I was invited to speak at a conference. I really didn't know what to talk about, so I pulled out my inaugural column. I hit the stage and told the story in much greater detail. The thousand or so written words turned into an hour-long keynote address.

When I completed my speech, I had the stage crew raise the house lights for questions. To my amazement, there were a lot of hands in the air. Everyone was interested in my long-winded story. They even had questions from 45 minutes prior, when I was just beginning my speech. They wanted more! I never thought people would find my story *that* interesting. After I left the stage, I had several people wanting to learn more, and everyone had the same question: "Do you have a book?"

That question pushed me into another deeper introspection, which led me to write The Venn Effect.

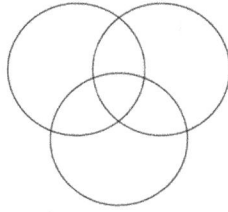

ONE
The Venn

M Y FIRST *FORBES* STORY LED ME TO a realization – I had written about my discovery of a personal Venn Diagram.

The Venn Diagram is a great way to describe my path in life. What may seem like convoluted and unrelated sets of information, is in reality, a blueprint of my experience. Those who are born entrepreneurs can probably relate to this concept. Our lives are a series of business endeavors: some so successful that they can spawn over-confidence, and some that result in failure and lessons learned.

The process can be repeated much like the directions on a shampoo bottle, but rather than "lather, rinse, repeat" it might be "start-up, success, sell; start-up, fail; repeat."

In a best-case scenario, the entrepreneur graduates from the "*fail*" portion of the equation. They will begin a new cycle of "start-up, *success*, sell, repeat."

Sometimes failures can occur in a very successful business. This is typically caused by late-term decisions that are execution centered.

In these cases, the equation might show "success, fail, success, sell" or something to that end. One must analyze the Venn to locate where their mid-term "fail" occurred, then take proper measures to protect their next venture.

I have created a specific path that illustrates this process in the Linear Retrospective Venn Logic diagram. In the LRVL diagram *(figure 1)*, one uses the information from each attempted venture, whether it be a success or a failure, and naturally moves forward without heavy analyzation of their experiences. It is just a list of information that may or may not transfer to the next effort to allow for personal progression.

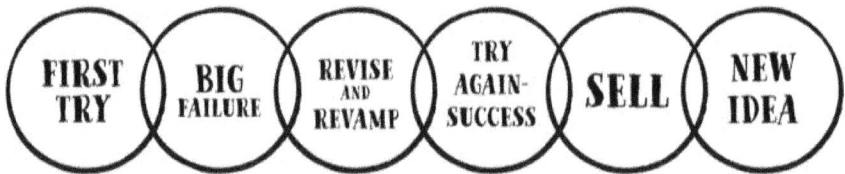

Figure 1—Linear Retrospective Venn Logic Diagram

Using LRVL is not an optimal way to start or operate a business if you desire significant, long-lasting achievements. Success can be gained and may be sustained for a period, but reliable outcomes are much less likely than if you use your experiences as a guide.

However, results can be improved by using a traditional Venn Diagram. By using a Venn Diagram, you can group your experiences: what worked, and what did not work. Then, using a relational diagram of successes, you can avoid practices that result in failure.

You can create a rewarding and sustainable company if you rely on your own Venn Diagram based on the successes and challenges of personal experience. This process begins with introspection.

First, it is important to understand what a Venn Diagram is and how it is created.

The Venn Diagram

This diagram represents the relationship of information between sets of data. It represents mathematical, logical, or unrelated sets of information pictorially. Generally, these data sets are represented within circles inside an enclosed rectangle. This is known as "the universal set."

Common elements of the sets in the circles are represented by and within the areas that overlap. (*see figure 2*).

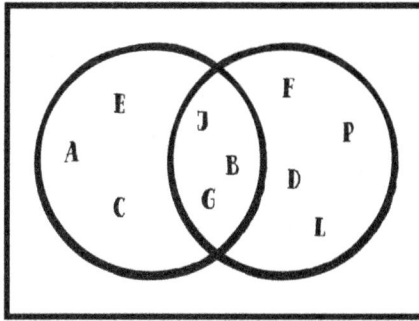

Figure 2—Universal Set

My Venn Diagram figure represents *my* life and thinking, which has not been a straight line. Your experiences will differ from mine, and therefore, your Venn may look nothing like mine. This is okay because we each have different paths.

If you look at mega-entrepreneurs like Elon Musk, Richard Branson, or Mark Cuban, you will find highly driven and focused individuals who differ from one another. These men have produced incredible results that are rightly celebrated, but if you look closely at a Venn Diagram, you will find ventures that didn't go well for each of them. These are the "failure" experiences that helped them learn and improve along their way.

In the Venn circles of *my* life, areas of seemingly non-related data overlap. These overlaps show focused areas where I've succeeded and failed, and why. Looking at my completed Venn shows a logical path forward based on my strengths and weaknesses.

My experiences reflect my personal Venn. In this book, I share both successes and failures, as well as the challenges I've faced along the way. Hoping these occurrences will help guide you in your personal quest, I've summarized my *Venn Lessons Learned* at the end of each major experience.

My story is one of constant motion, change, and transformation. I bore easily and am always looking for the next challenge, but I don't just drop a project and move on. I like to finish things and tie a nice bow, leaving a clean and proper finale to each chapter of my story.

That sounds easy, but I can assure you it is far from simple. Sometimes things end abruptly without a perfect, happy ending. This can be acceptable, but I have not always realized that fact until long after the fireworks have ended. Sometimes the circumstances surrounding an unhappy ending are beyond the control of the entrepreneur, and the sooner that reality is recognized and understood, the quicker he or she can move on.

Looking for my Venn Effect has resulted in a lifelong adventure, and I believe I may be only at the mid-point of my quest.

More About the Venn

The Venn Diagram is a tool created by John Venn around 1880. Mr. Venn wrote a paper entitled "On the Diagrammatic and Mechanical Representation of Propositions and Reasonings" for the *Philosophical Magazine and Journal of Science*, about the specific, yet different, ways to represent items or sets of items using diagrams.

In his theory, using these types of diagrams in a logic expression could help to identify similar ideas and qualities between available data sets, allowing identification of a common subset of information. In a Venn Diagram, one might take three different objects or experiences and place each with its own particular traits or data points within a circle.

After objects or experiences and their traits have been placed in each circle, the diagram shows the data that is shared in the overlapping area of the connecting circles. For example, a Venn Diagram can show a dog is like an alligator or giraffe because they all have four legs and teeth. And dissimilar because the dog has fur, and so on.

The Venn Diagram is a simple tool which can be used to identify otherwise hidden connections between objects or experiences that seem to be dissimilar. Essentially, it is a relationship diagram. This tool can be valuable in business to aid in the rational determination of similarities that can be acted on to further a goal.

These relationship diagrams can be used to assist both new and seasoned entrepreneurs, to better understand what works, and what doesn't, in an idea or in a business. Often the entrepreneur can get stuck in high-level failure without realizing it; they may have lofty or unrealistic target goals, basically missing the forest for the trees. It is important for any business owner, at any stage, to look critically at the information and then adjust target goals using the data presented.

Throughout my lifetime as an entrepreneur, I have continuously fine-tuned my efforts to account for past mistakes. Most of the time those around me may not even perceive the changes, but much like providing a course correction on a large vessel, small adjustments make for a more pleasurable journey.

Through all my lessons and growth, I have been able to create my personal Venn Purpose.

This is what I call: *The Venn Effect.*

TWO
Do What You Love

My Venn Begins

I STARED IN AWE AS WE APPROACHED THE beautiful old square rigger. It was a humid evening just outside of Savannah, Georgia. The day had been full of new experiences, interesting presentations, and intriguing investigations. This was our first chance to board the vessel we would use as transportation and a research platform.

Anchored off Devil's Elbow Island, the old ship was a mighty sight. Its sails stowed for anchor, it was rocking in perfect rhythm with the small swells in the protected waters of the May River near Hilton Head Island, South Carolina.

The view took me back to a few years prior when I was reading Robert Louis Stevenson's *Treasure Island*. The sight of the ship transported my young, impressionable mind to thinking that I might just meet pirates of yore on board. Sure, a far-fetched idea but a cool thought none-the-less.

The ship looked as if someone transported it from a distant time, or possibly straight off a Hollywood movie set. I was suddenly jolted from my youthful fantasy by the bump produced by the wake from a small runabout hitting our equally small transport boat. I realized that we were about to tie off and board the relic.

This was the real deal. My adventure was about to begin. What I was about to experience would be life-altering, and I knew it.

The Ship

It was the summer of 1978. I had never been on or even viewed something as grand as the *Barba Negra*. As we approached her starboard side, I was eagerly anticipating working with some of the biggest names in marine biology and oceanography. I was barely seventeen years old, but even then, I knew this was not an adventure that every kid who loved the "Undersea World of Jacques Cousteau" would have the chance to experience. I understood the enormity of this opportunity but couldn't possibly understand the extent of what it would mean to me decades later.

The *Barba Negra*, Spanish for "Black Beard," was an 1896 Barquentine square-rigger, 121 feet of finely honed and ornately carved wood. She was made in Norway for the purpose of whaling but had been converted in the early 1970s from a hunter-killer to a research vessel, devoted to the study of this graceful and often misunderstood mammal. When I boarded her, *Barba Negra*'s purpose was to record the sounds, calls, movements and mysteries of whales traversing the waters of the Atlantic Ocean.

The vessel was one of the last ships of her type constructed at the turn of the 20th century, as more modern means of marine propulsion were coming of age. The ship was the first of her kind equipped with a harpoon gun; however, that would only last for four years. In the early 1900s, she was converted to a cargo ship dedicated to hauling fish for coastal trade. She operated under sail only, until she was retrofitted in 1956 with a diesel engine.

As time wore on, a vessel of her type and construction could no longer compete against the newer, faster and more efficient ships available, and by the 1970s, her mission had taken a 180-degree turn.

When I boarded this grand ship, a captain who looked ready-made for such a vessel, or possibly a movie, greeted me. In fact, the *Barba Negra* and her captain had both been in a few movies. However, I did not know this, and as a naïve teenager; I fell for his act. He was an old, crusty, and seaworthy salt with all the wear of a mariner from the 1700s. His unkempt grey hair and beard screamed that he was not a shore-loving individual but one more suited as a swashbuckler from a time long ago.

The captain smoked a long pipe and grunted, rather than communicate in a fashion a teenager might find more inviting.

The stories shared by the captain were epic and probably a bit of sea lore but interesting none-the-less. His beard, pipe, and general demeanor made me want to believe everything he said, even though I occasionally suspected he was probably playing for his audience.

On our first meeting, he ordered me to grab a bucket and douse the deck with seawater to keep it seasoned and damp. He said the decking required constant application of seawater to keep the old ship in fighting shape. So, I started what would turn out to be a ritual of a kind, 24 hours a day. All hands – at least all *new* hands, took part in dousing the deck with seawater which was pulled up the side of the ship by a rope in an old wooden bucket.

The First Circle

I was born in the post-Great Depression, post-World War II age of my parents and grandparents. In the late 1960s and early 1970s, the business world was very different than it is today. It was the era made familiar to today's generations by the cable TV series "Mad Men."

During my upbringing, the formula for success was either you: graduated from high school and took a job at a big company, joined the military, or continued to college. All of these choices could provide a life with the prospect of stability, and even some benefits like a pension at the end of your career.

You were expected to work 40 hours a week, getting two weeks off each year for vacation. If you stuck with the company and advanced, this vacation benefit could grow to four or possibly even five weeks by retirement. At the end of your career, your company might give you a small party and if you were lucky, a gold watch or a retirement check.

I never fit this profile. I could not see myself working for someone else; it wasn't me. I preferred to call the shots, even when I was a kid. I longed to do something where I could create, grow, and build value. Something that would allow me to do big things; the things for which I had a passion.

A Shocking Reality

I have been told I was a "different" child. My mother often took issue with her ten-year-old, accidentally causing the power in our house to drop out due to my "tinkering" with the electrical system. To me, it was not "tinkering," but experimentation.

I recall her screaming my name at the top of her lungs, "Billy, what have you done this time?" She always called me "Billy."

"You know you're not supposed to play with the electricity—it could shock you!"

My mother was a master of the obvious.

I learned at an early age that an electrical fuse could be replaced, or an electric circuit breaker reset. I knew exactly what I needed to do to accomplish these tasks, hopefully without hearing my mother's screams, or feeling that all-too-familiar jolt of electrical current when I encountered something I should not have touched.

Experimentation taught me a lot, like how to terrorize my big sister by "tapping" her telephone. I figured out how to make calls on her phone line with only a transistor radio earphone and an old tape recorder microphone connected into the wall jack in my bedroom. I would experiment (or as my mother would say—tinker) with everything.

As my age grew, so did my "tinkering." I built a lab in our backyard shed, away from my mother's supervision, but not out of hearing range. You name it, I disassembled, reconfigured, or repurposed it. Nothing was safe. I mean nothing.

My experiments led to discoveries and lessons. If I didn't learn from the first jolt or small uncontrolled reaction (code word for explosion), I would repeat the punishment until I either broke something or got it right. I destroyed more than my share of electrical components and put out more lab fires in my youth than others do in a lifetime.

Those actions, along with the unintentional culpability of my mother—she was naïve to the chemicals she allowed me to purchase and experiment with—permitted me to grow as a scientist and engineer. But it was also those early encounters with unsupervised independence that caused me to develop bold and sometimes unconventional thinking.

A Salesman of Sorts

My first brush with entrepreneurship was by accident. I was ten or eleven years old, living in Las Vegas, Nevada. We had moved to Las Vegas from Los Angeles a few years earlier because of my father's work. He was an Air Force officer, so like any military family, we moved wherever the government decided they needed him.

W. K. (BILL) RADER

My mother returned home one day from a visit to my grandmother's house in Southern California with a huge box of plums. Hundreds of them.

I hate plums.

She told me if I didn't want the plums, I should take them around our neighborhood and sell them. So, I did.

I put the box of these hideous plums into my only means of cargo transportation: a little red wagon. This wagon would log many miles before I was old enough to drive.

> "This experience taught me that my expectations for results must align with my customer's desires (or demands)."

I went door to door with my first two employees: my younger brother and our neighborhood friend Brenda. We asked the person who answered the door to buy our "beautiful, Southern California-grown plums" for one penny each. We went to 50 or 60 houses in our neighborhood. At the end of our sales route, we had an empty wagon and pounds of pennies.

It was through this first official sales and marketing job that I learned an early lesson. You can offer a fair price for a good product, and you will still run into cheapskates—or people who want a better deal. Even though I priced these plums at a penny a piece, I still encountered buyers who wanted a better deal. It was painful to give up fifteen plums for a dime. The five-cent difference was a lot of cash to kids at that time!

I learned that in order to get the correct price for my goods, I needed to establish a floor price and an asking price right up front. The floor price is the absolute minimum price where I could cover all my costs and make a fair profit; the asking price is where I would start my negotiations. I learned the 'ask' should not be so high as to look like gouging, or too low, indicating a problem with the merchandise.

I enjoyed the fruits of my first sales experiment with a movie the next weekend.

This launched my journey. I was hooked. The idea of having my own spending money to do with as I pleased was an enticing prospect. I needed more of the green stuff—money.

I took my newly obtained expertise in door-to-door sales and went around our subdivision offering the services of my brand-new company, TAB Yard Services, named because we liked the soft drink *"TaB"* which was popular at the time. It also provided the added benefit of a professional logo and a recognized name. I owned some tools and hired my brother to help me with the jobs.

TAB Yard Services would cut, edge, and trim a yard (by hand) for $1.25. If you signed up for full-time service, we would maintain your yard every week for a set price. Note that sign-up was only a verbal "show up and do this each week" type of contract—not a legal one. By the end of our first summer, I pretty much owned the subdivision when it came to this service and had made a decent amount of money.

But more than money, I learned some valuable lessons. One of my customers, an older gentleman, held me to the highest of standards. He sternly let me know that if I were going to service his yard, it would be perfect. I was just naïve enough to think he was not serious about the perfect part. I was wrong. He wanted every blade of grass to be exactly the same length. Mr. Perfect (as I called him) would inspect the entire job after we thought we were done and inform me I would not be paid until we met his standards.

This experience taught me that my expectations for results must align with my customer's desires (or demands). It also reinforced that I must properly price any job or product. What this gentleman wanted was not a $1.25 job, but a gold-plated $5.00 job. I lost money every time I serviced his yard, not always in direct cash, but lost the opportunity to sell my services to others. I have taken this lesson with me ever since.

A simple concept which is often missed even by seasoned entrepreneurs is: If you provide a product or service of value, set a higher price than it costs to provide the product. If you have a service worth $5.00, profitable at $5.00, and you feel properly compensated at $5.00, then charge $5.00. You lose both cash and opportunity with every $5.00 job you sell for $1.25.

I could have cut five or six yards in the time it took to service Mr. Perfect's yard to his standards. Therefore, I had a loss of at least $6.25 in potential sales each time I serviced his yard.

My being an entrepreneur was very unusual during the early 1970s. My vocation made me different from my peers. While my friends were out playing and having fun, I was doing sales or performing services. I don't remember a time when I wasn't pounding the pavement, thinking up ideas, or looking for new opportunities.

As a teenager, I shied away from pursuing the standard jobs held by my peers. I didn't have a paper route or work at a fast-food joint. I never looked at my difference as a bad thing; I just wasn't content with the idea of a standard minimum wage. I wanted the wage of my father or his superior, not some skimpy hourly wage. I wanted to make a lot of money because it would allow for opportunity and control in my life.

Looking back, I guess I just didn't see myself as "cookie-cutter," someone who followed the pack. Granted, life could have been a lot easier had I just followed the pack, but this would not have amused me. I needed much more. I needed to solve, create, and manage.

The Undersea World

When I was twelve years old. I began watching television specials by the underwater explorer, Jacques Cousteau. It was the Cousteau TV specials that sparked my interested in scuba diving; it was fascinating.

I was adventurous and handy. I mimicked scuba diving in my family's backyard pool and built my own boat—even though I lived in the middle of the desert. It wasn't much, just a crude sailboat that I "put to sea" in our swimming pool.

I also took some risks, like turning a five-gallon bucket into a diving bell. I achieved this by weighing an inverted bucket with heavy steel exercise plates. With the bucket full of air from the surface, I would sink it into the deep end of the pool – my underwater habitat. Then I would dive into the pool and swim into my diving bell and be able to breathe while underwater.

From "The Undersea World," I learned the potential for expansion in the lungs when surfacing after taking a deep breath from the stale air in the bucket. So, when resurfacing, I always made sure to exhale completely when I left my diving bell, just like the Cousteau team did.

I don't think this was actually necessary because of the small change in depth, but I did it anyway—because Cousteau showed me the way. I made sure I read everything available about diving, and I started to purchase diving gear with the money I had made from TAB Yard Services. At $1.25 per yard, I mowed quite a few yards to buy a mask and snorkel. But with perseverance, I finally owned them.

During that summer, I was given the opportunity to learn about diving from my neighbor Mike Kaye. Mike was a US Air Force pilot, my Boy Scout leader, and best of all a certified scuba diver. He was the type of guy the kids loved to hang around because of all of his cool toys. From scuba gear to pinball, Mike had it all.

He often allowed a group of us to enjoy his toys while he either cooked or worked on projects. Mike even allowed me to test his dive gear in our pool—it was exhilarating. Mike saw my obvious interest and invited me to go diving with him in Lake Mead.

To my dismay, I was only allowed to watch him dive—he didn't strap me in and let me get in the water. But he did teach me how everything worked, how to set the pieces up and put them together, and how to put the gear on properly. Back in 1974, very few people owned the equipment to scuba dive, so accompanying Mike on this trip was a genuine opportunity to learn.

My Lake Mead "expedition" and solo experiences in our backyard pool had me hooked. Then my father received relocation orders from the Air Force; for me, exciting orders. We were being transferred to Florida. Yes, I was moving to the Gulf Coast of Florida—a place where I could seriously pursue my interest in diving!

Scuba diving was a rarity in the mid-70s. The concept had only been introduced to the consumer less than two decades earlier. Jacques Cousteau specials were regularly on television, which I religiously watched and fantasized about being part of his undersea world. I didn't know it at the time, but before the end of the decade, I would be a part of his exciting world.

Because of the times and his job assignments, I rarely saw my father during the first decade and a half of my life. It wasn't until he was assigned to Eglin Air Force Base in Ft. Walton Beach, Florida in 1976 that I really got to know my father. With this transfer, he had noticeably more time at home, even with his frequent work travel.

When we arrived in Florida, I was eager to learn to dive on my own. My father stood fully behind my becoming a certified diver and did everything he could to help me in the pursuit of my goal.

Shortly after our arrival in Ft. Walton Beach, he took me to the local dive store, *Ocean Sports*. This is the place I not only became a certified diver but where I learned about a crucial element needed in business: a simple premise that has stuck with me since our first visit to that dive shop.

As we were completing my first purchase, my father pointed out the motto of the store, boldly imprinted on the top of each receipt:

"Integrity before profit"

These three simple words greatly impressed my father. When I asked what this meant, he briefly explained the owners of the dive shop were more concerned with doing right than making money. This has stuck with me for over forty years and has been an underlying theme in every one of my enterprises.

My father's influence during this time of my life significantly shaped what would come. His teachings made a huge impact on me then and still do to this day.

"Integrity before profit"

My mother, however, didn't take as kindly to my new-found adventures. She had issues with the aquariums I kept in my bedroom and their inhabitants. I could understand her trepidation because I didn't have your standard goldfish—nope, I was a newly certified scuba diver and brought home saltwater creatures like an octopus and scorpionfish. Not pretty, but then again, remember, I was "different" according to her.

Aquatic Diving Company

With my new dive gear, my freshly minted Professional Association of Diving Instructors (PADI) certification card, and my father's support, I was off on what would become my first great adventure as an entrepreneur.

My first real business was literally "selling seashells by the seashore." As poetically funny as it may sound, selling seashells can be very profitable. It started with my first open water dive in 1976. I found a sand dollar shell in the Gulf of Mexico, off of Destin, Florida.

It had currency in its name. It was not a conch shell—it was a sand DOLLAR, and the seabed was littered with them. Dollars, there for the taking; and boy did I partake. It was like I found a Brinks armored truck spilled on the highway, and no one was interested, not even the driver. Better yet, I saw a market for them: the beach area was filled with artists selling painted sand dollars to tourists. I could scoop them up from the ocean floor and sell them to the large, existing market.

At first, I only "harvested" (that's what I called it) a few. I brought them home and spent my spare time studying them, doing research, and determining the best process to ready them for sale.

I discovered most people just soaked them in chlorine. This process worked to an extent, but based on a variety of conditions, it could result in a substandard product that smelled of bleach. The sand dollar, depending on the concentration of chlorine and time spent in the solution, could become extremely fragile and shatter when dried and handled. Sometimes it would be reduced to a pile of what one could easily call—sand.

I am somewhat of a perfectionist. I wanted the best product, one so good that the purchaser would pay a premium price for it. I wanted people to beg for more of my product. Reaching this goal required a lot of study, practice, and failure. I built a new lab in our backyard and got to work on a solution.

When I first started my business, I did what everyone said, "soak the sand dollars in a bucket with bleach." I had the same results as all the others: an end product that if handled a little too much, shattered and was worthless. I needed to ensure that a large-thumbed klutz could handle the finished product and that my sand dollars would hold up during shipping. Of course, we know all you need to do is mark *"fragile"* on a package, and it would be handled with kid gloves… Right? My sand dollars had to be sturdy to allow me to ship to other markets in the Sun Belt.

Therefore, I needed a superior product, and this would take research and prototyping. I didn't know what I was getting myself into, but I had my pride and saw that there was a lot of money to make, so I worked with my father to perfect a process. The result of all this work yielded a sand dollar that was not only clean, bright, and workable for the end-user, but was significantly stronger than those soaked in chlorine.

I found the concepts I had been learning in my high school chemistry class really helped. I analyzed the sand dollar: What was it made of? What could I mix that would do what I wanted? My goal was to clean the shell, but not adversely affect the end product's strength or appearance.

Through my analysis, I discovered I needed industrial strength chemicals for my cleaning process. Although I had problems locating them in my area, with a trip to my local library and a phonebook, I was able to find a supplier and purchase the required chemicals without issue. The drums of industrial chemicals arrived at my home and were quickly put to use in my production lab.

Next, I relied on my father's expertise in mechanical engineering. My plan was to treat the sand dollars with the correct type and concentration of chemicals, then to agitate them for a set time period, followed by a specific rinsing and drying process. I was taking what started as a fun hobby and turning it into a company producing a high-end product. It was important to me, and to my customers, that the sand dollars were of the highest quality, able to survive shipping, as well as handling by my clients.

My efforts at perfection were well received. I cornered the market with the highest quality, most readily available product obtainable. I even sold to raw product suppliers in other parts of the country.

I started by selling the sand dollars at art shows and then found my literal gold mine in an under-served industry: Jewelry manufacturing of the gold-plated variety.

In the late 1970s, gold sand dollar jewelry was the fad, and I owned it, at least the materials side. My sand dollars proved not only to be sturdy enough to be turned into art and sold by the seashore but were perfectly suited to withstand the plating process. I supplied the vast majority of the sand dollars used in jewelry to the gold-platers. They all wanted the Aquatic Diving Company product – my product.

I took great care to nurture and retain my customers. And I had more product available than anyone. No one could compete against me without a lot more effort than they were willing to put in. And, I owned the intellectual property—my process, which made for the best product.

I recall the day I met with a large gold-plater. He wanted all my product (an attempt for him to control the market). These guys were highly competitive, and they didn't like each other at all. They didn't want my product outside their personal control. So, I was schmoozed and courted by each of them in an attempt to win me over and cut their competitors out.

Each plater offered and paid a premium to buy what they termed as "all my product." They would place a sizable order for my entire stock on hand. However, I knew that I could supply each client just fine with my systems and supplies. So, I just scaled up operations and produced more. I made a small mint while supplying all my customers, covering all orders.

One plater even went as far as prepaying to reserve his portion of my product. This check would introduce me to a word I had never heard in my 16 years. After visiting my customer and collecting his check, I went home to enter the order into my books.

When I arrived home, my father had just returned from work. He was sitting in his easy chair, reading the evening newspaper.

When he asked about what I had been up to, I explained my recent order and showed him the check. His eyes lit up as he examined the check. It was larger than what he made in a month as a military officer.

He looked at me with a strange smile. One that said, *'I knew it all along.'*

He shook his head and said, "My God, you're an entrepreneur!

I looked at him a bit perplexed. This wasn't a commonly used term at the time. It was the mid-1970s—there wasn't a start-up community anywhere. Fresh-faced kids starting a company was in its infancy in the Silicon Valley and was years from being seen in the rest of the country.

I said, "A what?"

He looked at me with pride and said, "Bill, everything you touch turns to gold."

That was enough for me. I asked for my check back and went to my room to record the sale.

The Taxman Cometh

One item this newly minted entrepreneur did not slack on was keeping the company's financials in order. Not only was it important that I was fully licensed and insured but that I also paid my taxes on time. I researched the requirements and found addresses to where I could send requests for information on sales, withholding, and other taxes. I went as far as calling the State of Florida's main revenue offices in Tallahassee with questions and then sending them a letter to request the forms necessary for filing and paying all required taxes.

I expected to receive a letter with forms and instructions from the tax office. What arrived was not a simple letter and forms, but a visitor.

I was in school when Mr. Johnson showed up. It was a weekday morning in the early spring of 1977 when the government came knocking. My mother answered the door and was a little confused about why a man from the tax department was looking for her son. She told him I was in school and he could come back later if he needed to see me.

Mr. Johnson's office had received my letter and assigned him to follow up in person. He was amused to hear I was a teenager and in school. He gave my mother his business card and told her, chuckling, "We encourage kids to start little business, and there is no need for him to worry about or pay any taxes. He is way too young." He smiled and left, never to return.

When I arrived home to the news of both the visit and the words from Mr. Johnson, I was not only disappointed that he didn't leave the information requested but also a little incensed he took such a flippant attitude toward my enterprise.

"When in doubt, find the person in charge and ask for their direction."

Aquatic Diving Company was a real, licensed business with employees. I immediately thought about the potential long-term results of following his advice and could not come up with a favorable outcome. The way I saw it was in twenty years they would charge me taxes, penalties, and interest. I would be out a lot of money if I followed his directions.

So, I wrote another letter.

This time it was to the Florida Secretary of State. Sure, they could have turned a blind eye to this matter, but I needed to do things right.

Just as I thought, the State wanted my money and expected to be paid—regardless of my age. The Secretary of State's office sent me all the necessary paperwork and offered any assistance I might need to complete the forms. From that day on, I made sure I filed all taxes on time.

My first lesson in government interactions: When in doubt, find the person in charge and ask for their direction.

Back to the Barba Negra

I found myself an entrepreneur and a sand dollar expert. I spent a great deal of time studying these little creatures. I even built my own "sand dollar ranch" underwater. I knew my product; where they lived, what they liked, and how to harvest and process them. Because of the demand for my product, I had the money needed to pursue thorough research. So, I purchased everything written by, or attributed to my idol—Jacques Cousteau, particularly surrounding his adventures aboard the research vessel *Calypso*.

I bought the Cousteau Encyclopedia set. I would reference and read it regularly. I dreamed of going on an expedition with Cousteau. Cousteau was the biggest name in oceanography and marine biology, famous not only for his televised ocean adventures but also the invention of the Aqua-Lung scuba diving apparatus. I watched every one of his television specials, envisioning myself working aboard the *Calypso*. In school, I even took French classes in an effort to be at least a little proficient in his native tongue. Although I never became good at reading, writing, or speaking the language, I gave it a try.

I happened into my experience on the *Barba Negra* by writing a letter to the man himself.

In reading the Cousteau Encyclopedia, I found great errors with the information he presented on the sand dollar. I knew sand dollars.

I had studied them and recorded my findings. Sand dollars were my business. The information presented by Cousteau in his encyclopedia was at best, minimal and localized. The material was lacking, and I was confident the letter I sent to him had value. I used the power of the pen to take him to task on his statements. I based my letter on my findings, supplying the data I had been collecting to improve my product as evidence for my conclusions.

Aye Calypso

I am not a shy person, and those who know me know I always have an opinion. If I notice something doesn't look quite right, I do a little research and will often make the error known to the originator. This has been true of me for most of my life. I am not trying to do an "I told you so" or "look at me, you're wrong"; it's about fixing the problem and moving forward, so the correct information is available to others.

When I wrote the letter to Cousteau, I did not consider the enormity of telling the most famous and admired oceanographer of the century, possibly even all time, that he was "full of it." I didn't consider that one might climb the chain of command rather than going straight to the top. I wrote the letter, kept a carbon copy for my personal records, and sent it directly to Jacques Cousteau via US mail.

It is important when writing a letter like this to not only talk about the issue at hand but also provide an offering in kind. I did just that in my Cousteau letter—my "zero letter" of sorts. The offering I made was my data. This was the letter that started it all for me as a businessperson.

Sending this letter was my first experience in reaching out to people who most would consider inaccessible. It brought results, and it is something I continue to this day. Over the years since my first letter, I have written many others that repeatedly produced good results.

Cousteau—Project Ocean Search

To my surprise, I got a response from Cousteau. He thanked me for the letter and information and said he would address my observations in his next encyclopedia. But best of all, I was invited to attend research during the summer of 1978 with Jean-Michel Cousteau, Dr. Richard Murphy, and several others on "Project Ocean Search."

**"No matter the person, we are all human
and interested in learning. And all are
approachable when you share information or knowledge"**

The experience was life-altering. Working with and learning from these legends taught me a huge life lesson when it comes to people. No matter the person, we are all human and interested in learning. And all are approachable when you share information or knowledge. I have used this lesson over the decades to live what some have described as a "Forest Gump" type of life. I would not trade this experience for anything.

The Pitch

One day I witnessed something new to me. I was with Jean-Michel working on Devil's Elbow Island. A small boat approached the dock, and a couple of men jumped off and greeted us with big smiles. Jean-Michel looked a little puzzled but then remembered that he had agreed to a meeting with these men. A few weeks earlier, he had invited them to come for a visit while we were on the island to talk about their product.

Jean-Michel asked me to join them, so we sauntered down the island trail towards the old monastery we called home for this part of our adventure. The monastery wasn't anything grand, just a small group of buildings set in the middle, high area, of the island. It is there we met as groups, ate, slept, attended lectures, and just enjoyed each other's company during our precious downtime.

The two individuals we met on the pier were there not there for a tour or pleasure call; this was business. They wanted Jean-Michel and his father's endorsement for their product. You might think their product was some magic leap in diving technology; it was presented that way. However, it was nothing more than a new snorkel for skin diving.

I didn't know it, but what I was witnessing was my first business pitch. It was not a very good pitch from my point of view as a seventeen-year-old entrepreneur. And further, I don't think the two guys pitching their product were all that happy I was attending the meeting and taking part in the question-and-answer period of their presentation.

"Everyone is always selling something"

I might have been young, but I was an accomplished diver. I had multiple certifications and well over a hundred hours of diving experience. And, I was not shy about asking questions.

Jean-Michel deferred to my experience as if it were his own and let me question the men about their product. He even asked me for my opinion as they proceeded. I was caught up in the moment and didn't realize what was going on. My naivety towards being pitched, or sold to, was very obvious. However, I was also learning.

Business never stops. Be it as an explorer doing research or a salesperson pushing a used car on a local lot. Everyone is always selling something. As I came to realize this fact, I was able to understand better the stakes of the game for all those involved.

The endorsement of a Cousteau would be gold for these two entrepreneurs, and Jean-Michel understood this very well. I watched as he navigated the opportunity and then tested their product.

When the snorkel was placed into my hands, I nearly laughed. It was just a snorkel—the breathing tube one uses for breathing underwater when swimming near the surface. There are millions of these simple pieces of plastic all over the world, and it wasn't any different in the summer of 1978.

These guys felt they had invented a better mousetrap, and I am reasonably sure they may have. But sometimes better isn't necessary. And my feeling about their design was, '*Why?*'

I asked myself, "Would I buy this product? Would I recommend it for someone else to use?" And my response was simple. After testing and studying the device and listening to their sales pitch, my answer was a solid '*no.*'

But there is more to business than a great product. The endorser of the product would receive endorsement fees. For Cousteau as an explorer, the money from these fees partially funded his research.

Just like me, Jean-Michel played with the snorkel and was not convinced it was innovative. He handed it back to the salesman with a half-smile.

"There is more to business than a great product"

It was just another piece of plastic and rubber but with a fancy top and a swirl shape designed to limit the inflow of water when fully submerged. Any skin diver already had a natural way to clear the water out—just blow through it. There were already other snorkels that made this easier, but these guys were convinced of the superiority of their product, and they were seeking Cousteau's endorsement.

After some prodding from the salesman, we all agreed to test the snorkel. It operated as advertised, but exactly like any other snorkel I had used in the past.

At the end of the day, we took them to the dock and bid our farewells. I could tell that Jean-Michel was still not convinced of the need for such a product. However, I found the snorkel a year or two later while shopping for diving gear. There it was, hanging on the rack with his full endorsement. I chuckled as I looked at it. I am sure he justified the endorsement because it was safe, and it provided welcome research funds.

Time on the Island

During the expedition, we did many things on the *Barba Negra*, and Devil's Elbow Island. The group included scientists, a couple of post-doctorate PhDs, and summer interns like me. Everyone was focused on their work and learning most of the time, but there was time to play.

We were looking at sea life, from the salt marshes to the inter-coastal waterway, as well as farther off the coast. The studies were very interesting and time-consuming, but we found a little time to goof off while we explored the salt marshes. One time sticks out in my mind because, by the time we had returned from the marsh, no one was recognizable. In tidal areas, there is something called *pluff mud*. I remember the times vividly we would go out into the marshy areas during low tide to collect specimens for research.

While we were in the marsh, one thing led to another, and a war of sorts broke out—mud flying everywhere. The end result was a lot of extremely muddy people, pluff muddy. If you are not familiar with the consistency of this kind of mud, think paint. Very fine and very sticky. Everyone involved looked like the Creature from the Black Lagoon.

Each evening, whether we were on board the *Barba Negra* or on the island, we attended a lecture presented by someone on the project. Experienced oceanographers, biologists, and others would share information and findings from their past research expeditions. Knowledge flowed freely, questions were asked and answered, and conclusions were debated. It was a euphoric experience for me. I had never been privy to such a wealth of knowledge in a setting where I felt like a peer.

However, just as I was feeling like a scientist, reality crept back into my life. During the time I was away, I would get letters from home. It was in one of these letters my mother proclaimed that "I needed to return as soon as I could." She wrote that the business was out of control. I decided not to be overly concerned with the letter because there wasn't anything I could do to fix problems from my location. We had no phones available, just an occasional delivery of US Mail when someone went to Hilton Head Island for supplies.

A few days later, my concerns were put to rest when a second letter arrived, indicating that the problem was too many orders and not enough inventory. Not exactly the "out of control" I had anticipated, and a problem that could be remedied upon my scheduled return.

My First Brush With Media

When I came home from Project Ocean Search, I found that word of my adventure had spread across Northwestern Florida, and at least as far as Mobile, Alabama—enough to gain attention from the local press. Within a day of my return, I had a reporter at my door requesting an interview.

Emma Goggin was the reporter's name. She wrote a column entitled *Breezin' Around the Bayous* for the *Fort Walton Beach Playground Daily News*. She requested an interview about my adventure that she planned to title, *"Back From the Deep."*

I had no experience dealing with the press, even if it was a sweet lady writing for a local newspaper. She asked me to pose for "action photos" and asked a lot of questions. The next day when the article appeared in the paper, I was horrified. There were many inaccuracies and misquotes. She did, however, get a few things right. My main issue with her article was the content. Some of the things I only mentioned in passing she found entertaining and printed them.

For instance, I had mentioned that alfalfa sprouts were included as an ingredient with each meal served on the expedition. Then I flippantly commented, "by the time I left the island, I was mooing like a cow." I never thought much of the remark until I found myself in print with photos and observations, and more specifically, that offhand quote. As a teenager, one doesn't want this quote in their first news story, trust me. "Mooing like a cow" was something I was teased about in school.

A few papers across the panhandle of Florida picked up and published stories about my experience. I was greatly relieved when the embarrassing quote was not repeated.

I returned home from my adventure in the summer of 1978, more knowledgeable and a lot wiser. I was looking forward to my senior year in high school, already a successful businessman, an explorer, a marine researcher and, for a high school student, wealthy. I was making as much money as my father. I had a nice car, a boat, and a hefty bank account.

Life was good.

Selling my First Company

As I approached my school graduation, I looked toward the future. Sand dollars were supplying a good income, but this was a fad, and I knew it. I wanted to go to college and move into the adult world. I decided that I would need to sell the company when I graduated from high school the following spring.

I met with one of my customers. He was one of the most competitive individuals I'd had dealt with. He was a larger-than-life character who drove a new Mercedes sports car complete with a car phone—something nearly unheard of in 1978. He also owned a similarly equipped SUV. To me this was an impressive sign of success. He dressed the part too: full, dark beard, sunglasses, and an intimidating manner. Johnny was the person with whom I would strike a deal.

In addition to my product inventory, he wanted control of all the information I held and the methods I had developed. He wanted to ensure he could own all areas of my business so he could deny his competition my highly sought-after product. There was a lot of money at play here, and he was ready to deal.

Johnny thought his intimidating demeanor would cause me to be passive. But I was a businessman now, and his sunglasses, Mercedes, and attitude did nothing to intimidate me when it came to the deal at hand.

After a little haggling, I agreed to sell him the company lock, stock, and barrel. Everything: inventory, process, and methods; he would purchase all my trade secrets. I also agreed to help him set up and run the company at his location between my last semester in high school and the start of college, for a generous monthly consulting fee.

It was at Aquatic Diving Company where the first circle in my personal Venn diagram was created. I had learned one of the most important lessons in business at a very young age:

I often reflect on my lessons learned from starting, building, and selling Aquatic Diving Company. If you do not learn, you will repeat the mistakes you made in the past. If you take the time to learn and adjust, you can go much further in business. You can devote your time to always move your enterprise in the correct direction—forward.

In those early days, I learned the ropes of business under-fire and at a desk in the local library.

When I sold my business, I received a great price for my company. The profits partially funded my next venture several years later. I also bought a really nice Porsche.

Decades later, I would write a column in *Forbes* about becoming an entrepreneur.

Forbes—May 2017
How I Became A 'Professional Entrepreneur

Entrepreneurism is a journey, or at least it has been for me. What my journey has revealed over the years is that, much like traditional professions, there is a learning curve that you must respect and allow for, to assure yourself some reasonable amount of success.

Born to be a Professional Entrepreneur

Some say that people are "born" entrepreneurs or "natural" entrepreneurs. This may be so, as much as a doctor or engineer may also be born to be in their respective profession. However, most of us require education and training.

All professionals—physicians, lawyers, engineers, and accountants—go through rigorous training and education to master their respective fields. This is also true for professional entrepreneurs.

Think of this: Would you want the guy designing the bridge over that 1,000-foot gorge, doing so as his first project out of school? How about having your appendix removed by a newly minted doctor performing his first surgery? In both of these scenarios, you may be lucky, but do we want to count on luck in those situations, or skill and experience? The same holds true in creating a start-up business like mine, Efferent Labs.

The question then lies: How do I become a "Professional Entrepreneur"? One who has knowledge and experience to perform at the top of their game?

Most colleges and universities offer basic and advanced business courses designed to teach general, traditional concepts. However, even though these courses are necessary to learn foundational business principles, they don't teach you how to be an entrepreneur. They only provide a roadmap. You must also learn specific skills in a very non-traditional way if you seek to excel as an entrepreneur.

I have always felt that I was "born" to be an entrepreneur. As I have written about in other stories, I started early and without a lot of direction. Over time, I realized what I was and molded my skills slowly through a combination of experiential and traditional learning.

I tried traditional professions for which I was educated. While I excelled in my traditional journey from marine biology, through nuclear energy and electrical engineering, I was always looking for a way to take my education and experience and use it to create a thriving business that would make a real difference, one I could grow into a powerhouse.

I would find my way in the different companies I started along my entrepreneurism route, but it took a lot of work. Being a professional entrepreneur is not a 9 to 5 job. It is all-encompassing.

It's a matter of scale

You can be an entrepreneur, say the owner of a flower shop or a sandwich counter, and make a good living. You will provide a great resource to the community and provide jobs. Here you would be an entrepreneur small business owner and maybe have the opportunity for a more standard workweek. I applaud all those small business owners who can maintain a work/life balance while supporting the local economy and providing a service valued by the community.

Being a "Professional Entrepreneur" is a different commitment from that of a small business owner. Here I am speaking to those looking to scale an enterprise that produces hundreds of jobs and millions to hundreds of millions of dollars or more in revenues. Committing to be a professional entrepreneur is not a 9 to 5 job; it is a full lifestyle adjustment. You will work seven days a week, even when you do not think you are "on the clock." Twelve hours a day, or more, is not uncommon.

As a professional entrepreneur, you are always working, planning, and staying current with your reading. You even dream of your business. I keep a recorder near my bed so when I have that "idea" at 2 AM I can capture it before I lose it.

Perfecting your skills

So how do I hone my craft as a Professional Entrepreneur? I continually learn, I mentor others, and I share my experience through workshops and speeches.

When an opportunity to gain knowledge presents itself, I go, I learn. In fact, I have attended 10 universities and colleges over the past 30+ years. From the University of Southern California and Florida Institute of Technology to Harvard Business School. I attended to gain the background or refresher knowledge needed to maintain or perfect my skills.

These institutions, coupled with dozens of certificate programs and seminars, were used to gain knowledge and provide me with tools to creatively solve problems. Do you need to go to so many institutions of higher learning to be a Professional Entrepreneur? The answer is no. You can gain knowledge almost anywhere if you are open to learning.

When an opportunity to share my knowledge comes up, I jump at it. This can be a lecture, a panel presentation or a speech. I do a lot of preparation and work to provide a good experience for the audience. And, the research and preparation often teach me new approaches to the subject.

Do you need to speak and present to be a Professional Entrepreneur? Well, it definitely helps a whole lot. When relating to others, you gain a lot of knowledge. From inception and research through the actual presentation and Q&A, you will walk away with a deeper insight into your chosen subject matter.

This was my path, and I assure you it will expand, as I am a committed lifelong learner. I recognize my weaknesses, and I strive to shore them up by learning from experts, mentors, and professors.

Believe it or not, there is a "Professional Entrepreneur" certification created by very astute entrepreneurs. However, even a certification program is no assurance of success as an entrepreneur. It takes time, dedication, and work.

You will know when the time comes that you too can proclaim: "I am a Professional Entrepreneur," even without a certificate.

∗ ∗ ∗

My First Venn Lessons

In my early days, I learned that anyone and everyone is approachable—but it is important to have more than a story. You must share something of value without expectation of return.

- *Write a letter.*

    I have used this lesson often in the years since the "*Calypso* Letter." Reaching out in this way has brought experiences, introductions, and meetings, and even helped to build my "Billion Dollar Boardroom." I have gained many friends and countless opportunities—all by simply writing a letter.

    Today, you might be tempted to send an email – it is simple and requires little effort. But if you want results, sending a personal note the old-fashioned way, using the US Post Office, is where effort meets opportunity.

    Companies receive thousands of emails every month, some individuals hundreds a day. The bigger the person's stature, the more emails they receive—but very few emails reach their intended recipient. These high-stature individuals have staff who screen emails. It is almost impossible to know if your email has reached your intended recipient. You can sometimes catch their attention, but this is a rarity.

    I use regular postal mail. A well-crafted, high quality, hand-signed, and stamped piece of mail does several things. First, a person must perform the act of picking up the letter. They must handle the letter physically. This action creates a sensory connection – a physical and mental connection. Next, they must make a decision. "Is it something of value or a waste of my time?"

    Most act out of curiosity: "What is this all about?"

Triggering curiosity gives your letter a greater chance of being opened by your intended recipient, or someone close to them. Next, the person who opens the letter will at least scan it to determine its value—this is not something they can just click "delete" and never think about again. They are holding a physical specimen of your efforts: It is printed, typed, or handwritten; the letter is addressed and stamped; the postal system took the letter and delivered it to their desk. It smells of value.

Will the addressee read or respond? Your chances have been improved significantly by this sensory connection.

Personally, I have received a much higher response by sending letters rather than emails. If you want to get a message to someone effectively—mail it.

- The next lesson was the one my father pointed out at the dive shop: *"integrity before profit."*

It may seem like common sense, but many entrepreneurs get lost when faced with this concept. The most recent example is the CEO of the failed diagnostics start-up, Theranos. I have written about this company and its CEO in my *Forbes* column. Someone who might otherwise be a genuinely good person under different circumstances got caught up in pursuit. By all accounts, this person lost one of the most basic lessons of business—ethics. Some have written much worse things about her, but I will stick with this one basic principle: be ethical in your dealings.

- *Watch what you say and when you say it.*

When being interviewed, watch what you say and measure each response. If in doubt say, "this is not on the record" or "let me get back to you with that information." Media can be both beneficial and detrimental – depending on the way you present information.

- The last and most important lesson is, *"Do what you love."*

It is essential to be careful here. If you turn a hobby into a business, you risk losing what made your hobby enjoyable. It becomes a vocation rather than a vacation. Not all hobbies can be turned into a true business. However, if you love what you are doing, it feels less like work and more like a mission or a short vacation every day.

Take a moment to draw a circle and fill it with the things you love. Anything and everything. If it is climbing a rock or sleeping in on a Saturday morning—write down everything. Fill the circle, and if it gets too full, just make a list. Keep this information handy for future reference and do a similar exercise at the end of later chapters. This exercise will help you start the process of learning more about your personal Venn. You are now outlining your own Venn Effect.

More About Integrity

I wrote about Theranos and other companies with ethical issues in several *Forbes* articles. I include some of them in this book to aid you in understanding my thoughts on the subject presented.

My *Forbes* article *"The Theranos Effect"* was very popular, even winning the coveted "Editors Pick" award.

Forbes—July 2017
The Theranos Effect (Editors Pick)

As the CEO of a start-up life science company, I am always watching what is going on in my industry. During my company's Board of Directors meeting about a year ago, I was asked about the blood testing company Theranos. At that time, they were hot in the press with their CEO all over the media, a $9 Billion valuation and a reported $400 million in funding. This caught our attention, as it is unheard of in our space. The question asked in our meeting was how such a young start-up CEO like theirs could possibly attract so much valuation, investment and media attention to her company.

The only answer I had at the time was that Theranos must have found the holy grail of blood testing. I reviewed our product, something we have invested years of work designing and testing, with multiple issued patents—but could not identify a short path to market, just my stepped path. At the time I thought Theranos had not only secretly created an extremely advanced product but had also found a way to do it faster and cheaper than anyone else. What I didn't know then was that was only half the story...

At the end of the BOD meeting last year, I felt a little beat up. I was leading a talented team of scientists and engineers, developing something that had huge potential, but this blood testing company was kicking our butt in developing something that seemed to be impossible to our team. Although we are not competing in the same space as Theranos, we certainly will be compared to them as a start-up life science company.

What I didn't know at the time was their future. No crystal ball on my desk!

My Path

In the early years of Efferent Labs, I had assembled a well-seasoned board of directors and was able to make extremely good progress with our product. We have done so in a step-by-step process: building, testing, and validating one specific component of our product prior to moving to the next step of development. Although at the time of the board meeting, we were still more than 24 months from market, I felt we had done a great job with the science and engineering of our product, an insertable biosensor that uses the patient's own cells as the sensor. It is a ground-breaking product with enormous implications for personalized healthcare, but it must be developed carefully. We know that with such an advancement in medical technology, any misstep on our part could result in complete failure.

New Year, New Meeting

At our most recent Board of Directors meeting in May of this year, there was more conversation about Theranos, but this time the theme and tone had changed. Our strategy to validate our device along the way and obtain data before our next step was proving a very smart and prudent thing. I also had directed, due to my past experience, that all documentation would be fully compliant from the start, so as to be prepared for the eventual FDA scrutinization.

We are moving the ball forward every day. We may still have a way to go before our product is ready to be used by patients, but I devised a path to market that allows for investors to benefit along the way. These are early step-markets, where each step has a stop, and each stop has a market. For us, the first market is preclinical research. I am an engineer. Methodical might not be flashy, but it yields good results.

The Lesson

A lesson everyone in the life science industry should learn from Theranos—don't get ahead of yourself. We don't know the future for Theranos, or for that matter, my company Efferent Labs. My hope for both the companies is great success. However, the industry implications created by the hype of Theranos are already being felt. The Theranos Effect is not a good one, and it has hurt every start-up company in our space.

I think the main difference between myself and the CEO of Theranos, Elizabeth Holmes, is experience. I am much less interested in hype for my company and a lot more interested in proven results from our step-by-step methodology. I am not saying that she wasn't interested in results, but it looks to me that she was ahead of her company's outcomes. A CEO is expected to have optimism and excitement about their company and product, but this must be tempered with the reality of the situation so as not to unintentionally mislead anyone. Because I am seasoned (read old) in comparison to Ms. Holmes, I can hold my optimism for my product in check a bit better.

I don't want to promise before I can deliver. Yes, every company promotes its future products to some extent, but it is an absolute that the hyperboles not out-pace the results.

I am excited for the future of my products, but I want to ensure that my team successfully gets it to the people that will benefit from its use: the patients. To me the journey has always been about the patient, from the day I started Efferent as a patient myself.

We as patients deserve the very best healthcare. Maybe we can all learn a lesson here.

$$* * *$$

I Write When I Have Something Important to Say

My anger at the management of Theranos, and of other companies with whom I was very familiar, came to a head by early 2018. I had been following Theranos' antics for quite some time and had read about the charges of fraud that were finally being leveled against Theranos and its founders.

My outrage was pushed over the edge after visiting San Francisco a few months prior to writing the article and meeting a person with whose technology I am familiar. I noted this person was on a similar path as that of Theranos. Because of this meeting, I felt others might emulate Holmes' tactics in the medical technology field. This realization pushed me to write my next two stories about the industry.

Ethics is an important part of business, and I have seen people leave them behind in pursuit of the golden ring. Many companies come to mind. Enron is one, but to me the biggest offender is Theranos because it has directly affected the health and wellness of vulnerable people. The egregious actions taken by the management of Theranos caused a lot of stress for me personally in the advancement of my company, Efferent Labs.

Another CEO who made the news, time and time again, was Martin Shkreli of Turing Pharma. Mr. Shkreli, aka "Pharma Bro," displayed a pompous attitude and taunted the media. His actions caused a circus of events that eventually landed him in jail for securities fraud.

Things didn't have to play out this way for Shkreli. I'll admit, I understood some of his motivation for raising the price of the drug he had acquired. I also understood that he had put together programs, like many pharma and biotech companies, to cover a patient's out-of-pocket costs after the price increase.

It was clear to me he may have looked at the drug acquisition and subsequent raising of its price as a way to fund further research of other drugs. My thoughts on this may not have been popular. However, I understood what I assumed he was trying to accomplish.

I believe he executed things incorrectly, possibly due to the nature of his personality. I cannot be sure of this; however, the fact remains as of the writing of this book, he is sitting in jail. I don't know all the details surrounding the security fraud case for which he was convicted, but I feel strongly that if his actions were more ethical and less antagonistic, events for him could have fallen a different way.

I wrote about ethics for *Forbes* in the series of articles that follow:

Forbes—September 2016
The EpiPen Debacle Coupled With Theranos
And Turing: Is This Industry Broken? (Editors Pick)

The bad and ugly

As the CEO of a life science company, I have watched with concern the debacle of the Mylan MYL -0.07% price hike on the life-saving EpiPen, and with absolute contempt for the (debatably nefarious) actions of Martin Shkreli of Turing Pharma. You remember this guy, pumping his profits citing research and development costs, while patients suffered.

Couple these actions with the issues created by the problems at Theranos, and you have created a crisis of epic proportions in an industry that is working hard to help people while balancing a return for its investors.

Is the industry broken?

This leaves many asking the question: Is the healthcare industry broken? In some ways I would chime in with a resounding yes, but in most others it is a solid no. We have, as an industry, created some of the most beneficial advancements for the improvement of mankind. We help millions of sick and suffering people every year heal and live better and healthier lives.

The advances that the life science industry continues to make help everyone, me included.

Not all that long ago there was no real treatment available to better the lives of patients, like myself, who suffer the effects of multiple sclerosis. Today there are many choices that help millions stay the progress and reduce the suffering caused by this chronic condition.

The industry as a whole is not broken.

The issue created and not fixed

I can't help but notice the onslaught of advertisements from Mylan in recent days. This is an obvious attempt by Mylan to recast and redirect their story. However, from my view it is more an attempt to refashion the current narrative away from the poorly thought-out issue it created for itself and for the industry as a whole.

The fact stands: they made a very bad choice, and on the heels of other bad choices by a few individuals, and have created a mess for the industry at large.

There is no debating that the product manufactured by Mylan is of great benefit to those in need. It has been a lifesaver to many, as shown in the now constant television advertisements. But the idea of changing the game with a huge price increase with no real explanation other than "pricing it to better reflect the benefit" is an insult to the patients as well as to the insurers. It is not only bad PR but more importantly, bad to the patient who has been a loyal consumer.

Then, after a lot of pressure created by public outcry, Mylan back peddled with a cost reduction of 50% on their generic version of the product. This is a clear statement to the world they overpriced the product and have been shamed into reducing the price.

Government chimes in

I also take issue with the US government. In recent days, the White House has chimed in painting all the life sciences with a broad brush by calling the entire industry "greedy". Senators are calling for hearings and the industry is being painted into a corner based on actions of a few.

This broad brush is not fair and is more problematic than problem-solving. I have been in the life science industry for some two decades and have seen a lot. The overwhelming of what I have witnessed was good. I have observed hard-working scientists attempting to solve some of the most daunting medical mysteries, while others work equally hard to make sure the discoveries of these brilliant scientists make it safely to those in need.

This alone defines an industry that works and works very well.

My viewpoint as a CEO

In the not-too-distant future, I will make pricing decisions on the products my company is developing. Our products will be of great importance to patients, and it is vitally important to not only offer a safe and effective product but also do so in the most ethical manner I can. One of the goals I have is to price the product right the first time.

Value-based pricing is the answer

Pricing is harder than you might expect, as there are a lot of considerations to take into account, not the least of which is insurance and Medicare reimbursement.

I am sure I will end up using a value-based approach to pricing. It is the fairest and best-accepted practice in the industry.

Is there value in the Mylan device? Without question. It has saved many lives and is of absolute need. However, when many years after the first market, the company dramatically increases the price is questionable at the very least, and has caused a greater uproar in and against, the industry.

Had they considered and used value-based pricing to start, they may not have experienced the current issue.

The industry is a repetitive target of politicians and others, and the last thing we as an industry need is another perceived money grab caused by a few bad players.

My viewpoint as a patient

I personally am the beneficiary of the great work of Pharma and Biotech companies and have had my life made much better these great companies and medical device and health analytics companies. I am not only an industry veteran, but I am also a patient, and I look at things through the eyes of both.

As an industry veteran, I can attest to the great difficulty in taking an idea from the lab bench to the bedside. It is expensive, very expensive.

Therefore , pricing products correctly is of utmost importance from the get-go. The product must be priced to cover the cost of development and manufacture, but also have a profit high enough to pay for research and development of other discoveries, while returning a dividend to the investors.

Something not mentioned in the media is the pharmaceutical pipeline funnel. This is information that needs to be shared with the public, so people can understand the high cost of creating the products that help us so much.

The fact is, a thousand products may be produced and tested before we find the one that works. It is expensive and time-consuming. Pricing takes this process into account as the research and development costs are huge.

As a patient, I want a product that has been thoroughly researched, manufactured according to the strictest of standards, and priced so I do not have to take out a second mortgage to live. To this end, the pharmaceutical companies I have benefited from as a patient work to make it easier for me to pay for and use their product through programs that cover copays, or in some cases cover the entire cost of the product. Patients just need to ask.

The industry

Pharma, biotech, and medical device companies are not evil. The actions of a few are casting a negative light on hundreds of thousands of professionals and the companies they are proud to work for.

Modern medical science has increased the quality of life for millions, but as a society we need to better understand the value of great science and medicine.

Ask a patient if the healthcare they are receiving is worth the cost—and I would argue that the overwhelming majority is grateful for access to the best medicine and healthcare in history. I know I am.

$$* * *$$

Forbes—March 2018
The Truth Behind a Pitch: An Entrepreneurial Lesson from Theranos

Each year I have witnessed many "pitch" contests and participate investor pitches in locations across the United States.

If you're not familiar with the investment pitches and contests, think ABC's "Shark Tank" television program, but with industry experts and/or investors asking the questions.

Having given countless pitches myself, I feel that it is very important to sell the vision for your company, its capabilities and the potential return on investment. I want to give a full and accurate picture of where we are today, and where we are going to be tomorrow. I work to sell our vision, but also make sure I am clear and accurate with my words and descriptions.

However, I have noted over the last year that selling a vision and being entirely truthful can sometimes prove a difficult task for some entrepreneurs. Either through being naïve, overly optimistic or in some cases just flat out deceitful, some entrepreneurs I have witnessed may just get lost in their desire for success. I have witnessed them stretch facts to fit their goal.

Sometimes they leave out the "science" in a life science company, or the "tech" in a tech start-up. Watching pitches as an educated and experienced engineer, I have seen pitches that defy the laws of nature, but have the entrepreneur selling the vision as real and here today.

Sadly, sometimes investors or contest judges can be caught up in the hype and encourage the fantasy rather than call the entrepreneur out for explanation.

An entrepreneur doesn't have to look far to see their future if selling a fantasy.

In the case of the unicorn start-up Theranos, they had incredible investment, over $700 million, resulting in a $9 billion valuation, a huge hiring spree, and a lot of deceit from selling what we now understand, as a technology that did not exist.

One of their employees put the hype and reality together, noted the fiction and then reported to the government and then the Wall Street Journal. Thus, the downfall of a unicorn was witnessed around the world.

This leads to a big question—why? Why would people that I am sure are good and honest, stoop to the level of publicly espousing falsehoods to win a competition, or gain investor funds?

Well, in many cases I think it is because they either just foolishly believe in their dream too much and have blinders to the facts or are naïve to the reality of their efforts. Either one is a case screaming for a reality check, and investors or contest judges should do just that.

But the bigger issue might be an attitude it doesn't matter. That it's okay to fudge the facts if it means getting ahead personally and being a business "celebrity", able to climb a ladder to the next, bigger opportunity. Some may look to jump while on top after taking money from a few wins and leveraging it for a bigger position elsewhere—leaving the company and investors to topple behind.

Investors often say they bet on the jockey and not the horse. Well, you can have a Kentucky Derby winner as your jockey, but if he is riding a child's hobbyhorse, he will not win. Just like selling fiction in a start-up, the entrepreneur and investor will not win.

In my view the entrepreneur is vitally important, but the technology must be there, and if it's not there yet, disclosure is a must. The technology being promoted by the people presenting it must have some semblance to reality. At times the investors may have glasses fogged by a great pitch and don't think to ask the questions that really mean something.

It is ultimately the responsibility of those investing to root out fact from fiction, however in some news stories over the last couple years, this was shown to be more the exception than the hard and fast rule of investing. Many people have lost a whole lot of money, and more importantly in the case of Theranos' patients were put at risk.

Theranos leaders have also had charges of "massive fraud" leveled against them. After watching this develop over several years, I can only believe that this story will not end well for anyone.

It is time we look at the television pitch shows as what they are entertainment. We need to bring the pitch back to less of a show and more an exchange of information.

When we get away from the game show style pitches, the investor and entrepreneur will both win.

✳ ✳ ✳

My First Lesson in Business Made Me A Writer

These articles show that I can restrain my outrage and still drive home valuable lessons. I included them in this book to allow a deeper look, not only at my experience but also my motivations. It is important to me that an entrepreneur stays true to one of my earliest life lessons: "Integrity before profit."

A lack of personal integrity will follow you in business and in life. I have witnessed this many times throughout my journey. Placing integrity before profit will also follow you, but with healthier results. Time and again, I have been tempted by those with less than good intentions to alter the grounding instilled in me by my father. I have never wavered from his foundation. I strongly encourage every entrepreneur to hold fast to this principle.

I am very passionate about the harm caused by entrepreneurs like those I mention in my stories. My anger resurfaced in a similar story I wrote for *Inc.* a few months before the "Truth of a Pitch" appeared in *Forbes.* By the time the *Forbes* piece went to press, the empire created by Theranos' CEO was already crumbling. How badly, I didn't know at the time, but an investigative reporter from the Wall Street Journal did and wrote about it on several occasions.

His writing not only exposed the fraud but also hastened the fall of the company.

For me, writing is just a way to share information of interest to me personally. I know that I have gained both fans and critics over the years, and I am okay with this fact. It proves that my writing causes people to think.

Over one and a half million people have read my published thoughts over the years, and although this is not a huge number considering the world's population of potential readers, the number is big enough for me to take notice. The key to my writing, my business leadership, and life in general is candidness. Basically, what you see is what you get.

When I place my thoughts on paper, I always write about topics that interest me. From there, I attempt to share in a way that provides data and entertainment. Perhaps along the way, even give the reader some useful information.

I've written about ruthless and deceitful entrepreneurs to highlight contrast. I desire to let those who may be wondering know that there are honest and straightforward entrepreneurs trying to create something good. Some of these companies have affected me in more than one way: personally, as a patient; and professionally, as a business leader.

So, I have used my available platform to share the lessons I have learned along my path to those following behind me.

THREE
Anchors Aweigh

I T WASN'T LONG AFTER MY FIRST BUSINESS exit that I started my next adventure in life. I attended the Florida Institute of Technology, then promptly enlisted in the United States Navy. Life was looking promising after my success with Aquatic Diving Company. However, I needed a new challenge. The Navy put me through Nuclear Power Engineering School and then assigned me to a submarine.

As was the case for everyone in my class, before graduation, I put in a request to be assigned to a specific naval command upon graduation. I asked to be assigned to a fast-attack submarine stationed in San Diego, California.

A fast-attack submarine is a class of naval vessel with a schedule that is not set in stone; it sees several ports-of-call each year. The crew on this class of submarine did very interesting and secret things. I really didn't know what they did or why, how, and where they did it; it was the mystique of the adventure that captured my imagination. Therefore, this class of boat was on the top of my list.

However, it was more important to be assigned to a location that was near my girlfriend. I hadn't seen a lot of her during my schooling because I was located across the country most of the time. So, I needed to convert letters and phone calls into personal visits through a situation that gave me greater availability—even though I would have an unpredictable schedule.

But the needs of the Navy are almost always opposite of the service member's desires.

I ended up being assigned to the USS James Monroe (SSBN 622). The James Monroe was a nuclear ballistic missile submarine, also known as a "boomer." A boomer carried enough firepower to make the vessel one of the largest nuclear powers in the world. The boat's home port was Holy Loch, Scotland, a far cry from the beautiful shores of San Diego and any chance to move the relationship with my girlfriend to the next level.

The submarine and the location gave me another great lesson in life: Sometimes you must go with the flow.

A boomer has an entirely different mission than that of a fast-attack boat. The boomer carries an arsenal of nuclear weapons that, if launched, would cause enough destruction to drastically change the world in a few short minutes. The upside of being assigned to a boomer as opposed to a fast-attack was, the boomer had a regular schedule. The boat and crew were deployed for a strategic deterrent patrol, followed by a rest and relaxation (R&R) period—also known as "off-crew"—located at our home base in the United States.

"Sometimes you must go with the flow"

I served at the height of the Cold War. When everyone else thought we were at peace in the 1970s and 1980s, those on patrol knew the reality was much different. We were at war, just not a formally declared one. Tensions between the United States and the USSR were at an all-time high when I showed up, and we knew we could be called upon at any time to do the unthinkable.

During this time, President Reagan ratcheted up efforts to bring the Soviet Union to their knees. My submarine's role as part of the nuclear triad was an integral part of applying that pressure. Our operations helped keep the people who were on dry land, breathing real air, safe and sound.

Life on a submarine is not for everyone. In fact, it's hardly for anyone. It takes a unique kind of person willing to lock themselves up in a giant steel tube for months at a time, breathing man-made air, while manufacturing drinking water from seawater.

I was one of those people, living a life that was filled with a strict and regimented schedule for several months at a time, then allowed temporary freedom during the off-crew period to do mostly as I wanted.

Service on a submarine can be both monotonous and terrifying. Usually, the monotony lasts a long time with spurts of absolute and abject terror just to keep you on your feet. You quickly get lulled into a rhythm. And knowing there is nowhere to go anyway, you just go with the flow.

We didn't complain much. We did our job, always hoping to return to the same world we had left.

I spent much of 1985 through 1987 underwater, on patrol aboard the James Monroe. A schedule that cycled approximately three months at sea, followed by roughly the same amount of time off-crew in Charleston, South Carolina.

Yes, Charleston is as sweet as it sounds. It is a beautiful southern city full of charm and history. It is a great place to return after months of sunless days and starless nights underwater. It was a place that allowed me to recharge.

The off-crews were a time when the boat's second crew, in our case, the "Blue Crew," would take over for us, the "Gold Crew." When our time on the patrol cycle was up, we would leave the boat with the Blue Crew and fly back to the United States for a couple of months.

During this time of rest and relaxation, I was easily lulled into believing that I was a civilian again. I worked on my ideas for businesses and even attempted to create one or two. Then off-crew time expired, and I found myself being jetted back to Scotland to play yet another round of hide-and-seek with the Russians in the North Atlantic Ocean.

The off-crew period was not enough time to do much if you were an entrepreneur. Right as I stuck my toe in the business waters, I found myself headed back to the deep waters of the Cold War.

On a submarine, we had very few choices of to how to spend our time. By design, it is a very contained industrial environment. We were there to support the boat and its mission.

The days underwater were set at 18 hours rather than the normal 24 hours. This was due to the way watch shifts were designed—6 hours on watch, 6 to 12 off, and then repeat. Drills, training, and free time were also part of the schedule, whether you were on or off watch. There was no sunlight, no stars, no commercial radio, and no television other than a few old videotaped movies.

When I was working, it was all-encompassing. I was the person who controlled the nuclear reactor that provided power for the electricity and propulsion of the submarine.

While on watch, my team was focused on the power plant. When not working, I was studying, taking part in drills, or sleeping. In fact, even when I was on watch, I did those things—all except sleep. There was precious little time to dream in my time off, but when I could dream, I did.

There was no way to research while sitting under hundreds of feet of water in the middle of nowhere. I had a "Walkman" brand tape player, a book or two, and a few friends to keep me entertained when we were not on watch. And we did this for three months at a time: no contact with the world, contained in a metal hull, submerged and alone, waiting to react if called upon.

Our job as submariners was to go to sea and hide, awaiting our orders. We were ready to launch our payload on orders from the commander-in-chief, the President of the United States. This action would likely have resulted in tremendous damage to hundreds of thousands or even millions of people. It was a heavy weight to bear as a 24-year-old. Luckily, we were never tasked with launching a weapon in a case of aggression or defense.

History shows these efforts worked. By the time I left the submarine service, my boat was scheduled to be decommissioned and converted to scrap metal; at the same time, the Berlin Wall was tumbling down.

It was while on Strategic Deterrent Patrol that I had a "Eureka!" moment for my next business.

Although I was thousands of miles and months away from home, I had to think about something. There was little in the way of reading material: no newspapers or periodicals, much fewer business books. Aside from an occasional paragraph of world happenings or a message from home known as a "family gram"—a Wells Fargo-type telegram that each crew member was allotted—we had no real news. All we had were the books we brought with us or those available in the ship's library (which was the size of a kitchen cabinet).

I was able to scratch my ideas down on paper. With nothing else to do for entertainment, I focused on what I would do when I returned home.

I kept detailed notes on my ideas. However, without resources to investigate or study, I ended up answering questions in my mind rather than relying on research. Big mistake!

Eureka!

My eureka moment was the idea for a mobile quick oil change company. I named it MobiLube. In my mind, this would be the answer to every busy person's needs—a quick oil change on wheels. Our tagline was,

"We come to you!" The idea seemed ingenious to me, and in a lot of ways, it was.

I spent time both on and off watch concocting the idea. I remember clearly, sitting in an area known as Auxiliary Machinery Room 2 while on patrol, thinking about the way this company would be designed and marketed. Planning and scheming on the "how's" and "why's."

I knew I was solving a problem that many people had. They needed auto service and didn't have time to take their car to the local dealer or the drive-in quick-lube. During one of my off-crew cycles in Charleston, I conducted limited market research using a small survey. After reviewing the results, I knew I was on to something of interest.

I created the initial business plan for MobiLube. As I got closer to completing my contract with the government, I became serious about MobiLube. Soon after my discharge, I rented an office in Charleston.

I had known Charleston was a medium-sized test market for several ventures in the past, so I felt that the demographics represented a good place to start my company. I tacked up my sign and went to work.

MobiLube had a tiny office with a couple of desks, one computer and a communications center containing a phone, a paging transmitter, and a fax machine. I squeezed everything into less than 200 square feet: tight but effective. I was used to being squished into roughly 18 square feet on a submarine, so our office seemed large and luxurious.

If the company was going to be successful, I would need to use the latest available technology to control the operations, plan out the daily routes, and maintain schedules of appointments. Efficiency was essential to maximize throughput. Our trucks needed to be servicing clients, not driving to them. Timing service activities was one key to making a profit.

At the time, there were few tools available for a company like MobiLube. Our technology consisted of an Apple IIc computer with a color dot matrix printer and the "smart" pager of the day—a one-way, text-only system. This was considered very innovative and high-tech in 1987.

Using current technology to make a cutting-edge and profitable company seemed like a sound idea. I was well versed on the computer and with technology in general. Since I understood some mechanical engineering and was an educated electrical engineer, I felt the last part—servicing the cars—would be trivial. I had actually changed my car's oil once or twice in the past, and it didn't seem all that difficult.

Next, it was time to staff the company. Professionals needed to do the actual service. My initial challenge was finding the right people to hire. The people would need to have experience with auto servicing. However, I could not afford to use ASC certified mechanics and be profitable. I would need basic service technicians: people with experience in rudimentary oil change service and knowledge of basic automotive maintenance.

During the planning for MobiLube, I knew it would be important to incentivize technicians, which was similar to the pay structure in the drive-through service business. I planned to use the technicians as the first line of sales: I rewarded them with bonus payments if they upsold services, if they could sell to other clients needing service while at a scheduled location, or when they increased their turn per hour rate.

I scouted local oil change companies for potential employees. If someone were to have knowledge in and understand the day-to-day operations of my company, a quick-lube specialist would be it. I placed an ad in the local paper that was designed to grab the attention of these potential employees.

Within a week, I had several inquiries about the position. One applicant was a top technician at one of the larger quick-lube chains. I invited him to my office and asked a lot of questions. I needed to learn more from him than he learned from me. I asked him to provide input about potential issues that might come up in our mobile service concept and his solutions to them.

I knew from our conversation, I had found someone who could help develop the company from a technician's viewpoint. I offered him the lead technician position a couple of days later. He accepted my offer and quickly recruited the best people he knew to join us.

We were off and running. But soon we started to sputter like a car running low on fuel.

Our work started by focusing on sales and marketing. We needed to get our name and idea out to the public.

I created and produced a fancy jingle and quirky advertisements relating to issues caused by not servicing your car or by waiting for service in a greasy building. I paid for spots on local radio stations, and for print ads in the newspapers. We conducted radio campaigns and used direct mailing services to hit the rest of our target audience.

We worked weekends conducting live on-site promotions with radio and television stations. The live promotions would include oil change contests and give away free and discounted services to promote our company. We spent the rest of the week running our trucks from customer to customer, learning our business by working our business.

The saturation advertising cost a lot of money; however, without the multi-point marketing campaign, we would have had a hard time reaching and educating the consumer about MobiLube's services. In 1987, this *was* social media—the only way to get potential customers to interact with us and buy our product.

Issues Start Early and Oil Flows Downhill

It didn't take long for issues to start flowing in faster than the oil was flowing out of MobiLube. We were a small, proof-of-concept type of start-up. Even with my early work, the planning was not great. In fact, it had major gaps. One of the biggest problems became clear very early and was one which could have cost me a considerable amount of money, or even put me in jail if it had ended badly.

Things went awry shortly after we set up our service warehouse in a commercial/residential storage facility. Everything in the company seemed perfectly set up and organized. We had a warehouse with shelves stocked full of tools and supplies. We had secure storage for everything we needed for day-to-day operations, including the oil. Our trucks could be stored there when not in use, and we had most of what we needed to support the weekly scheduled services.

In our normal service, we would drain the oil from the customer's vehicle and place it into a truck-mounted waste oil storage drum. The storage drum would slowly be filled during the day, then be moved off the truck and into the storage facility at night. When the waste oil drums in storage were full, a contract service would come to our facility and remove the oil, providing a receipt to show the chain of custody for the hazardous waste.

Sounds simple. However, as the saying goes, stupid is as stupid does. We had a major gap in disaster planning and failed to consider a leak or worse, a spill of waste oil. We just didn't think about it. Our storage warehouse was a large rented unit. Some of the adjacent units were full of the other storage customers' personal property. Our planning did not include a retaining system for waste oil in the instance of a leak or spill.

And as luck would have it, we had a leak within days after starting our official operations.

The storage facility management called us reporting an issue in our unit. My employees hurried to the building and found we had a significant leak. The storage unit was nearly level, so there was an even disbursement of waste oil to surrounding units. We immediately tried to stop the spill and began to clean up, but the oil managed to reach an adjacent unit before we could fully contain the issue.

We were lucky. The unit next door did suffer some damage, but it was minimal. I spoke to the owner of the items and reimbursed him for his minimal losses. The spill was cleaned, and we erected a barrier system to ensure that any future leaks would be contained and not cause another problem.

We were investigated by local officials who could have caused us great pain, but the actions we took to remediate the leak and prevent future problems satisfied the government. With a warning, we were back to work.

Other issues started to mount on the service side of our operation. When we took orders, our call center didn't ask the customer if the vehicle to be serviced was operable. In a standard quick-lube company a person drives in for service, so we assumed that if we received a service request, the car was drivable. The phone operators would take basic information, like the type of vehicle and location, and digitally dispatch a service vehicle.

The public has an uncanny way of rapidly finding flaws in a business plan. A few people quickly realized they could try to have us change the oil of their old clunker, one which hadn't been moved from its location in a decade or more, and my service technicians bought it hook, line, and sinker. Since my technicians were incentivized on sales, they didn't like to say "no," they just attempted to do the service even if it meant moving a dead squirrel or another strange obstacle out of the way to do so.

In one instance, I was called out to a service location where things were going badly. My technician had started to remove an old, rusty oil filter from a broken-down 1972 Mercedes parked in a field. The customer was pushing him to just "change the oil." The engine and car were in terrible shape, and the filter was rusted and deteriorated. The technician wanted the incentive pay for turning a car rapidly and went for it. He attempted to remove the filter, and it fell apart, leaving a hole for oil to flow out of the old engine freely. The customer demanded the oil change and insisted on us repairing the damage caused by the attempted removal of the old and deteriorated oil filter.

When I arrived, the angry customer was threating everything from calling the police to suing us for a new car; none of which was even close to happening from my point of view. I helped the technician fully remove the filter and replace it. He then refilled the oil, and we left.

The car should not have been touched in the first place, but I did not have written operating procedures in place, outlining what should and should not be serviced. The technician was only interested in the sales incentive. If we had failed to complete the service, I would have more than likely been liable for an engine repair or overhaul on a broken-down car.

This experience made it obvious that we had some major holes in our operation. As soon as I returned to my office, I started creating Standard Operating Procedures (SOPs) and employee training materials.

From that point forward, SOPs have been an integral part of every one of my businesses. They are some of the first things I create for our operations.

FOUR
Do What You Know!

I WAS NEVER A PERSON WHO PERFORMED MY own vehicle maintenance. I didn't know the ins and outs of the simplest of activities—changing oil—let alone the issues that might crop up when changing the oil in, for instance, a 1972 Mercedes diesel. Nor did I fully appreciate that each car and engine required a different type of oil and air filter, or that the amount of fluid required for a proper oil change could vary by vehicle. I just figured it was an easy task to accomplish and put a standard price on the service – a one-size-fits-all price. I may have changed my oil a couple of times in the past; however, this lack of detailed knowledge turned out to be a big problem.

Servicing a 1972 Mercedes is one thing, but if you add in the fact that the engine uses diesel fuel, you must add time and cost to the maintenance. When we initially advertised our services, our first customers were those looking to cash in on my ignorance, and they did just that. Many of our initial service calls were from people with every conceivable issue a car could have. It was like they could smell a sucker and a deal from a mile away.

We had calls from people who owned cars which had not been moved from their backyard in years. They wanted us to basically overhaul their car's engine for $19.95. In the case of the Mercedes, the oil filter was so badly rotted that the minute the technician touched it, the filter disintegrated. The customer knew there would be issues and tried to hold us responsible for his rotted engine. On top of everything, fixing this problem took a lot of time, shattering our three turns an hour rate, which was the requirement for the profitable operation of the service truck.

With all the problems we encountered in our original business plan of targeting consumer services, I determined large fleet accounts would be where profit and growth could be obtained. We pivoted our operations to support large fleet clients. However, even with commercial fleet accounts, there were issues. One of the main operational challenges was the logistics of having the client's vehicles available when our trucks were on site.

These large customers required their trucks, just like ours, to be out in the field performing their required service. One of our first accounts was a large utility company. We had to arrange a rotational schedule that permitted a set number of trucks and cars to be available on our service days. This was doable, and we could make it work on our end. But because the needs of our customer's clients prevailed, problems with their vehicles' availability persisted.

Vehicle availability aside, the biggest issue for me was the payment schedule. These large clients paid invoices on a net-90 term. This payment term means that the customer issues the payment 90 days after they receive the invoice for our service.

Therefore, we would need to carry all costs: materials, consumables, employees, and overhead for at least three months. If we could negotiate better terms or find a way to finance the costs for at least six months internally, we could work out of the debt incurred during start-up. I calculated it would take roughly twenty-four months to create stable cash flow. After this, the net payment requirements would be much less onerous.

However, the fact was we were a bootstrapped business: a business that uses limited upfront resources to start, using revenues to build and grow the operation. Getting paid on time with a net 30 term was required for our success. We could not float large amounts of money for three months—it was unsustainable. We loved the big contracts, but even with them, we were still a new company and could not qualify for bank financing to sustain us until our financials stabilized.

This was not something I had thought of when creating our business plan. I made a mistake a lot of young entrepreneurs make. I led myself to believe in the "Field of Dreams" approach—if we build it, they will come. The problem I faced was the people who showed up in our field of dreams to play were those like the Mercedes owner. I made the mistake of allowing the on-site service technician the latitude to make his own decision when it came to working the job or calling for advice. The mistake of not having procedures for this aspect of the business proved costly.

Next, I did not consider fleet accounts upfront. Selling to these types of clients could have been a perfect way to bootstrap the company. Had I started with commercial accounts, I could have used the money I spent on consumer advertising and chasing broken down heaps to cover operations while waiting for the payment from the fleet accounts. By the time we pivoted to target this type account, we had no cushion to allow operations to continue while we awaited payment on the net 90 terms.

Factoring and The Kiss Of Death

With all the issues I was facing on the financing front, I reached out to a local business advisor. He introduced me to a small venture capital firm (VC firm), who immediately had an interest in my company. I did not know of venture capital and was not versed in the requirements they might have or the information they would want to review. The two people I met were not much older than myself, but they had a lot more experience on the money side of deals than I did. They were very enthusiastic about what we were doing and quickly made some recommendations. The VC firm suggested they would be interested in moving towards backing my company if we could grow at a faster rate.

They encouraged me to talk to a friend of theirs who could provide financing using my receivables as collateral. This idea sounded like it could really make the difference for our operation and save the day. I made the call to the recommended individual. He explained that he could help small companies like MobiLube when banks would not. He offered to do something I had not heard of before: "factor" my receivables.

Factoring is a word used to describe the selling of the money payable to you by your clients to a private finance company or individual for a fee, plus interest. Using a factoring company, you can get the money you are owed by your customers, minus a service fee and interest—immediately.

In my case, I would be responsible for the entire invoice plus an exorbitant interest rate, and a chargeback fee for any factored debts left unpaid after 60 days. A complicated formula, but they assured me that there were rarely issues and the cost would be contained.

In many factoring situations today, terms are negotiable. If you can afford the fees and other terms, it can be a good way to finance a new venture. However, I would caution that there is a risk of getting caught in a factoring loop and draining profits to pay the fees. In a factoring situation, it is very important to have a sales margin that will support operations, pay all the costs associated with factoring, and have a sufficient profit at the end of the day to maintain and grow operations.

Factoring was not a good idea for a small start-up company like MobiLube; our sales margins were too low. But I had few choices left. I factored my receivables, and after paying the debts owed by the company was left with no money to continue operations. Even with a way to continually factor my receivables, I could not remain in business. My need was greater than the payment of debt at this point. I needed additional funds to cover operations beyond the factoring deal. However, the funding company was only willing to offer a one-time deal for existing receivables, not an ongoing operational agreement.

I received a phone call after I took the factoring deal. The caller suggested that I meet with the people from the VC firm at my office.

The two people I had originally met came to my little office and sat across from me with a third person who was unknown to me. They knew all of my issues because I told them everything hoping they might be able to assist with our immediate problems. They suggested it was time to transfer ownership of the company to them. They said they would make sure operations continued, the employees were paid, and it was the best deal I would find.

I was shocked and angry with what I felt was a shakedown. But at this point, I knew more about them. These people, who had been encouraging me and suggesting they would invest if I would follow their directions, were large holders of ownership in a regional quick-lube company. This fact had not been disclosed at any time in our prior conversations, nor did I know anything about this until well after our initial meetings. In fact, as I recall, it was the factoring contact who let this information slip when we were talking on the phone.

The new deal they were proposing would leave me in the same position I was in personally, only they would own the entire company and all its assets. What they didn't know was that MobiLube had no other debts other than the operational debt. I was the largest single investor, and the only other investments were small.

Thinking back now, I probably could have struck a better deal—one where I would have been paid enough to cover my investment or more. I might even have been able to negotiate a good exit. But I was young, inexperienced, and pissed off. I let my emotions get in between me and a potential buy-out, even if it was small.

I reminded them we had a non-compete agreement in place and then invited them out of my office with less than kind words. In our agreement paperwork, they could not use the information I disclosed to go into the mobile oil change business. In hindsight, I really don't think they wanted to anyway. They were probably just working to remove competition.

I used the money from the factoring deal to ensure that I shut all operations down in an orderly fashion and in compliance with my guarantees, both personal and business. This left nothing for me, and at the end of the day, I had used all my savings and credit to cover the company. I would eventually dig out of the hole I had created, but it would take much time and effort.

MobiLube is an example, failed as it was, of bootstrapping a business. Again, bootstrapping is the use of limited upfront resources to start a business, using revenues to build and grow the operation.

Although starting a business using the bootstrapping method is feasible and can work, it is important to have a lot of data in hand prior to launching. I wrote an article about bootstrapping for *Forbes* and have included it for your benefit.

Forbes—July 2016
Running On Empty: Lessons Of
Bootstrapping A Business

Bootstrapping is the process of using limited personal resources to get a business started, then reinvesting profits to grow it without the aid of outside investors. If done effectively, this is a great start-up strategy—especially as you answer to no one but yourself.

The values in bootstrapping:

- It's all on you, so you will work even harder for your success.
- You manage time more effectively.
- It forces you to focus on what matters.
- You own it.

You can still make progress when your cash indicator is near empty.

With the exception of my current company, I have bootstrapped every business I started in the past. For Efferent Labs, it is about scaling a different kind of business. The only way for me to do this is to take on outside investment.

At the beginning of Efferent Labs, we were bootstrapping everything. We didn't start to take on outside investment until we were a winner in the 2014 43North competition. The boost provided by the $500,000 investment that came with the win, allowed us to supercharge our efforts and gain outside interest.

Stretching, Grants and Freebees

To get more with less EBAY has been a great friend of the company for purchasing and selling equipment. We have also been able to stretch our dollars with matching grants. This type of grant is a little easier and quicker to obtain than a federal grant and is usually funded around economic development efforts in a city, region or state.

In a matching grant, you supply an application that justifies your need. If successful, you are provided a match (1:1, 1:2, etc.) that allows the completion of a specific project over a timeframe. Even with the required matching money, these grants are powerful financial tools for a start-up. Most sponsors do not provide the cash directly to your company, but instead require that you directly pay your match money for them to manage. They, in turn, process invoices for the services, or supplies and equipment required, and pay the venders directly. This reduces headaches when the tax season approaches.

When we needed expensive market research, we looked at a local university. The University at Buffalo is the largest institution in the SUNY system and has a great MBA program.

W. K. [BILL] RADER

We presented our needs to a professor and a team of graduate students who worked on our study as their class project. The team's work would have cost us precious cash; however, using student resources only required us to use some of our time to guide them and review their findings.

Another method many start-ups are successful employing is the use of stock options for compensation, or even goods and services. While this is trickier and poses an additional risk, it is a very common tool. However, you must exercise caution, as issues can arise in determining the price and/or value of the options. This is where some investment in legal and financial services is critical. All parties suffer if the price is not set correctly.

This brings us to some key reflections from my bootstrapping experience:

- Be resourceful. Look outside the standard "corporate" way of doing things.
- Get out of the kitchen (or garage, or office) and network. It's generally free, or very low cost, and you might find a person with the information, equipment or resources that can help bring you to market.
- Spend every dollar as if it were your own money, and as if it's your last.
- Never buy what you can borrow.

These days, being an entrepreneur is all the rage. But despite its glamorized appeal, remember that the path to success is grounded in this hard reality—it always comes down to the Benjamins.

$$* * *$$

Lessons Learned

My original idea was to have a company that could provide automotive service at a time and location best suited to the customer. I thought it would be good to accomplish oil change services like those done at a quick-lube, but also tune-ups and other basic services, all at the consumer's location.

On the surface, it seemed like MobiLube would be a big hit. The idea was fairly simple—I mean, how hard is it to do these services? Well, I found out the hard way it was a little more difficult than I had anticipated.

When I conceived the idea – on board a submarine in the middle of the Atlantic – I didn't have the resources available to do the necessary research into the auto service industry. I sketched things out on paper, coming up with ideas that looked very good at the time.

It wasn't until after I created the company and had issues that I reached out to an old and trusted advisor. She was my first mentor outside of my father. Her help to navigate the closing of my company and her expertise as a CPA helped me greatly.

I learned several lessons with MobiLube. The first that comes to mind is:

- **"Do what you know"** I was not a person who maintained my own vehicle. I always relied on professionals to take care of the simplest tasks. My ignorance had left me with the impression of simplicity. When planning the company, I didn't look at the basic operation of the service at the level required. I made assumptions on paper. These assumptions proved wrong.

- **Undercapitalization.** With a service business, the bootstrap option for building the company seemed perfect. This was a bad assumption for our service-related business because it was not a business to business (B2B) operation from the start. Had I started as a service company for large fleets, even with the net 90 payment terms, we would have had a greater chance of being successful. The turns per hour were more than double that of a consumer-based venture because our clients' vehicles were sitting right next to each other. Our overhead was equally reduced for the same reason. In addition, our clients would often request add-on services. But best of all, our commercial clients were more forgiving and understanding should something not go perfectly.

- **Test your business plan.** My business plan was flawed from the start. My time spent on marketing and the high cost of consumer advertising took valuable resources from the company. The money spent on advertising could have extended our runway substantially, allowing for continued operations and meeting the net 90 terms of the commercial client.

- **SOPs should be created and used in all businesses from day one.** It is crucial to the operation and control of a business that a set of instructions detailing how to do all the important operational tasks in the company is current and available. What seems simple and mundane to you, might not be to someone who comes behind you. The SOPs will also provide proof of control of your operation should an issue come up that requires either a legal remedy or a governmental action. It is important in these instances to have your procedures written and available. Using SOPs provides the answer to many questions. They also provide for continuity of business should someone leave the organization.

- **Bootstrapping is not for all.** Bootstrapping can provide for a low upfront cash investment for starting a business. One of the key items to think about in any business is the burn rate. This is the amount of money, month over month, that the company will consume to operate and grow. It is a major mistake to think any business will be 100% cash positive from day one. Most of the people I have met whose bootstrapped business failed had assumed profitability from day one. In my case, I had money to operate and assumed a cash profit per-service, as well as a 30-45 day, turn around on invoices. This was a flawed assumption and quickly manifested itself when I accepted the large fleet accounts. However, even with the net 90 turn around on these accounts, the business was doomed because of the high cost of early customer acquisition. We could have held on with our pivot to servicing fleet accounts, but we had already passed the point of no return as far as available cash to make the new model work.

- **Just because you have a eureka moment, it does not mean you will be successful.** If you can't spend the time validating the idea and researching the best operational methods, you should hold off starting operations until you do.

- **Find a mentor early.** Preferably in the idea stage. Find a trusted individual who can help you in those areas where you are not familiar or have no experience. Then, heed their advice. Even if they are just lending an ear from time to time, a mentor can be better than a large bank account.

I wrote about mentors in my *Forbes* column:

Forbes—October 2016
How This Entrepreneur Found Great Mentors And Advisors

Mentors, advisors, friends and family have all had a prominent effect on my successes in business. The people in my life that have had the most influence did so in a selfless manner.

I have been very fortunate to find great people at the right place and at the right time along my journey, who were eager and willing to help me learn and grow.

As I look back at three of the most important influencers to me as an entrepreneur, I note that the best mentor entered my life through their own accord and at a time when I most needed them.

How can a person recognize and accept the efforts of people willing and wanting to assist? There is no magic formula. You sometimes just need to step away from the path you have laid out and use the input from others.

My first mentor offered her help when I was a young entrepreneur—still a high school student struggling to build a company while my peers were playing football.

A close friend's mother, an MBA and budding CPA, initially read and offered input on my business plan. She helped me to better understand key concepts in business as I started my first company.

After that, I often sought her counsel. She provided me with a voice of reason and one degree of separation. This separation allowed for an honest and non- emotion-based evaluation of the situation.

Her unbiased input caused me to take a step back from my sometimes stubborn and steadfast reaction to a problem and allowed me to make sound decisions to grow my business. This also allowed me to grow and mature as an entrepreneur.

We celebrated my victories and worked out issues together. Her influence on me as a person and business executive was a key part in my life until her untimely passing from cancer.

I have had many mentors in my life, often at the same time. From my father, also an MBA, to my current Board of Directors, I have always appreciated good counsel when solving complex or sticky issues.

My father would talk to me every week offering advice, celebrating my wins and dissecting my losses with me, until his recent death, also from cancer.

These counseling needs seem to line up at a steady pace for an entrepreneur. The value of a seasoned and involved board of directors can be very valuable if properly used. I know the plague of entrepreneurism often meets with an unwillingness to admit the need of advice, but as a lifelong entrepreneur, I can assure you that seeking advice and counsel is more often the secret of success than not.

How I found My Mentors and Advisors

In some cases, as with my first and most influential mentor, our relationship started by just being in proximity and having a good personal relationship.

However, networking brought one of my most recent advisors. I met him in a chance meeting at a business event.

He approached me and started a conversation. I, being skeptical as to his interest, asked about his business. He stated he was a lawyer. I immediately stepped back, held up my hands in a defensive move and said, "I don't need any more lawyers!" He looked me in the eye and said, "I don't want to be your lawyer, I want to be your friend." I believed him, and a friendship was born.

He went on to become a key business legal advisor in my latest venture until his passing from cancer.

Throughout my journey, losing people to cancer has become a relentless theme. These three great mentors are just a few of the people that have assisted in my efforts and their loss is a huge reason I am now in a business concentrating on helping people to combat and beat this and other horrible diseases.

Sometimes you just need to listen

My advice is to first connect with a person wanting to help you, then listen to them and heed their advice. Sounds simple on the surface. If you listen, do otherwise, then go back and complain because the results were not what you wanted or expected, you won't ever get to a relationship that will be of benefit for you or them.

As an entrepreneur, life is great when you make good decisions. However, attempting to do everything on your own is often more foolish than brilliant. Therefore, listening to experienced and educated advisors who are truly dedicated to helping you succeed can be the difference between a horrible failure and a rousing success.

Often an entrepreneur may not listen to the counsel provided and go it on his or her own, disregarding all advice.

I have seen this many times. That might be a good choice sometimes, but more often than not, it can be disastrous.

Having a clean, clear eye on an issue can help in many ways. Using advisors that are a degree removed from the problem is often a key to success in solving an issue.

How Can You Find Your Advisors?

My advice to finding advisors is networking. I have written about this before and I cannot overstate the power of a network for an entrepreneur. If you stay put in your garage/ office/basement—you will not put yourself in the proximity of great people with vast amounts of experience. Advisors who may turn into your mentors are out there looking for you.

Get out, participate and look. Befriend and get to know people at networking groups and always be on the lookout for that special person you both click with, who has a deeper background or different parallel knowledge than yourself. You want an advisor that will challenge you, not agree with you all the time.

* * *

The Venn Lesson Provided by MobiLube

It should be obvious from everything that occurred with this venture, that failure was inevitable. It should also be evident that at that time I was missing a major element of my Venn:

This basic premise is a key to success in any type of business. Knowing the nuances of what you AND your staff are going to be engaged in, and how to prevent technical and client issues is the major lesson from MobiLube.

I learned many other lessons with MobiLube, but the know-how lesson could have averted at least some of the major headaches presented early in this short-lived venture.

Had I sought out advisors and mentors earlier, I could have avoided a lot of pain. The knowledge of our company's offerings, the basic how-tos, was lacking from the start. I could have answered a lot of questions and saved money had I just asked an advisor at the start.

I have taken all the lessons I learned at MobiLube to heart. In many ways, I have used them at each company since.

If you experience failure in your Venn quest, it does not have to be the end of your world. My Venn was just taking more shape with the MobiLube debacle.

Three good things came out of my MobiLube experience though: I met and married a smart and pretty girl—Millie, and added her sweet two-year-old, Olivia, to my home. And, after a year, we welcomed our own child, Jonathan, to our family.

Always remember, it's not how many times you fall down, it's how many times you get back up that defines your success. Just because you have a failure—it doesn't necessarily mark the end of your entrepreneurial journey, it just opens a door to a new beginning.

FIVE
Timing is Everything

A FTER THE HUMBLING COLLAPSE OF MOBILUBE, I took
time to lick my wounds, recover financially, and start anew.
My new beginning found me as I was reviewing my past experiences.
I took a position as a control system engineer at an engineering firm.
The position provided me a way to use my education while expanding
my experience by consulting in many different industries. It also
allowed me time to think and recharge.

Failure is never an easy thing for an entrepreneur to accept.
However, if failure is approached correctly, it can provide a clearer
vision for future ventures. The first lesson I learned as an entrepreneur
was always to do what you really enjoy doing, or:

DO WHAT
YOU LOVE

I thought long and hard about this directive. It was one of the most important lessons I took away from Aquatic Diving Company. I loved what I did when I owned that company. I loved almost everything about it. From the adventure, to the freedom, to the cold hard cash. Doing what you love can be both personally and financially rewarding.

However, I learned an even more important lesson from my complete and utter debacle at MobiLube:

The knowledge part is very important. In fact, it is crucially important!

Think about this for a second: you may love playing the piano, but the fact you can play chopsticks does not make you Beethoven and yields very little chance for your success as a professional pianist. It takes knowledge, talent, and practice. Knowing how to play the piano is critical. In fact, know-how is required!

Tinkering My Way to Success Again

I started experimenting with a relatively new technology after the fall of MobiLube. The technology had been around for the better part of a decade, but it wasn't widely known outside of hobbyists.

The technology involved a system using a power line communication protocol (PCP) from a company named BSR. Their engineers were working to remotely control lights and appliances and created a method and protocol to do so. The X-10 company came from the tenth experiment at BSR.

The engineers wanted to see if they could use the existing electrical wires in a standard home to control lights and appliances remotely. In their tenth experiment, they had success sending signals out on a home's electrical wiring and receiving these signals using a remote plug-in module to a light's power switch.

BSR used this successful tenth experiment to create a product and eventually the X-10 company. X-10 is a basic way to use existing electrical wires in a house to transmit 'on-off' and 'dim-bright' command signals to and from the X-10 modules. This allows a homeowner to remotely control lights and appliances without the need to install additional wiring.

The X-10 modules are less expensive than adding wiring to a house to do exactly the same thing. Basically, a light switch is replaced with a new "X-10" switch. The homeowner uses a small control module that is plugged in elsewhere to control the X-10 switch, thus enabling them to turn a light on or off remotely.

It is a simple concept in standard use today, but in the 1980s this would have required the addition of wires. One of the features was a wireless remote control, like a TV remote. With the remote, one could turn lights or appliances on, off, or even dim the lights. With the addition of simple software, they could create a schedule to do even more things automatically.

In the mid-1980s, I started to follow the early industry of home automation. The idea of automatically turning lights and appliances on and off based on events or time was intriguing to me.

I was first introduced to the technology in 1983 and believed it had great potential. I experimented with the equipment for a few years and created interesting software to control the X-10 modules. I invented hardware to control items like the electric water heater in my own home.

In 1990, I decided to start my next venture, Hybrid Technological Systems, Inc. But by the time I incorporated the company, I had shortened the name to Hybrid Technical Systems, Inc. Even though

I reduced the overall name by four whole letters, it was still a tongue twister. So, for short, we called the new company HT Systems.

I learned that a company name really matters. I chose the original name because we were creating hybrid systems and products. It would have been much smarter to have a company name that had a more familiar connotation to what the company did and to convey that to the potential customer.

When naming a company really think hard. Longer is usually not better. Be concise. Make sure your target customers understand what you do by your company name.

This lesson in correctly naming a company has stuck with me over the years, so much that I wrote a *Forbes* column about this item alone:

Forbes—September 2016
Is Your Company Name All That Important?

Why I changed my company's name

A year ago, I made the choice to change the name of my company. We had been known for several years by another name (note: I do not mention the name as I only want you to remember our new name) and changed our name to Efferent Labs, Inc. last year. The idea and desire to change our name did not come easy or without cost. I wanted to have a name that better reflected the products and goals of the company, rather than a name that was hijacked from another company. At the time I chose the original name, I owned a well-established company, Raland Technologies, and used the first part of its name (Raland) because it was easier to quickly and cheaply adopt.

However, confusion occurred. Potential investors would look up "Raland" online rather than searching for our full name and finding the other company. I was questioned by potential investors if they were being asked to invest in both the other company and the new one. This confusion convinced me that I needed to change our company name, and I got my Board of Directors approval to do so in late 2014, just prior to our win of the 43North business competition. Although I had the approval to change our name, when we pitched at the competition, we would need to do so using our old name. We took too long to make the change, and the wheels were already turning on the events publicity.

At that point, I was confronted with a major decision. We won the competition under the old name but still needed and wanted to change. The amount of media attention afforded by winning the largest business plan competition in the world would be enormous. Interviews and write-ups would offer great publicity. I chatted with my Board and we decided to wait on the name change until 6 months after the 43North competition, giving us time to best capitalize on the old name, and then change our name when news cycles caused by the win died down.

Did other founders have similar issues?

I wondered if other companies also went through a similar dilemma when deciding to name or change the name of their company. I reached out to two start-ups that were getting ready to or recently had changed their name. I had dinner with Dr. Irfan Khan a month ago, and he mentioned he was about to change the of his company. At the time we spoke, he was in the same situation I had been in two years ago.

He is founder and CMO of a start-up company, Circuit Clinical (formerly Empirican PRN), and a recently announced semi-finalist in the 43North competition.

I also reached out to a newer start-up that only launched in July of this year. Joe Ulisano started what is now Kick Ad Marketing, in July of this year. Originally known as SocialHire360, they quickly changed their name after launch. Within 60 days, they had not only recognized a need to change, but they did it.

The decision

Unlike both Irfan and myself who are life science related, Joe recognized and acted quickly. Then again, he is in the marketing space to start with, and recognized the potential for loss if he did not act quickly.

At dinner, Irfan told me a story that harkened back my thoughts to 2014. I asked what prompted his desire to change the company's name. His response was eerily close to mine—he needed a name that made sense for his company's growth.

This is the exact same reason that Joe changed his company's name.

This resulted in a lesson for naming a start-up company:

Spend time to do it right the first time, and when your first choice fails—and that may just be the case:

- rethink (re-think your choice)
- rename (Chose and implement)
- remind (Remind your customers who you are, and of your name change).

Methods are different but results the same

Irfan used a professional agency for his company's name change. Using professionals helped his process out greatly and resulted in what they were looking for, with all the heavy lifting done by others.

His results: a complete turnkey name change.

Joe hired a consulting company to assist with his company's name change, then quickly fired them and worked with his internal team to determine the right name and how to accomplish the switch. After all, they are marketers.

For me, it was a lot different. We did not use professionals. It was a yearlong exercise of jotting down ideas, shooting them over to my co-founder and thinking about them, sometimes for hours but more often days or weeks. Every idea was wrong for us—until that fateful day when we found the right one and knew it. Efferent Labs had meaning, and it fit our company. To us, that was our golden pick.

We then hired an offshore logo designer (read cheap, very cheap) for branding, and local website designers.

Our results—pain, suffering and savings.

Their take-away

I asked Irfan and Joe two key questions about their experience:
What did you learn and would you do it differently?

Irfan: "I think what made the process easier is that our agency, 15 Fingers, took the time to understand us deeply first, before making any recommendations. It also helped that none of the founders acted from a position of emotional attachment to our original name. The team began by asking: 'Is this the right name for the company we're becoming?'"

"Empirican was originally just a play on the idea of being empirical—which is a good thing for a clinical research company to aspire to be. But over the last two and half years, we grew into a fully integrated enrollment and retention solution for Sponsors and Contract Research Organizations and we needed a name that captured that. Circuit Clinical reflects the company we've become and gives us a stronger foundation to build on as we grow."

Irfan: "The rebrand itself has been a relatively painless process—I attribute that to the excellent guidance we received from our partners at KMG Capital and the quality of the work done by our agency, 15 Fingers. The one thing we could have done differently is: ask the question "do we need a new brand?" sooner. That's likely just a product of founder bias, as people tend to like the ideas they start with a little more than they should!"

Joe: "If I had to do over again I would keep it simple. I tried to get too specific with the first name and it ended up being confusing. I'd make sure the name has "wiggle room" for service adjustments or service additions to leave room for growth. With our current name, we can grow into a full-service ad agency. We just happen to be starting with social. Our name, core offer, and plan is simple which makes it much easier to scale, train, and project into the future."

My takeaway

For me, the questions are shorter but similar. What did I learn? If you have a few dollars, outsource the process—and as stated by Irfan, ask yourself the question: "is this the right name for the company we're becoming?"

What would I do differently—again, an almost mirrored answer—do it sooner.

**

HT Systems

I had decided to start a company where I really enjoyed the work, and in an industry where I had education and expertise. I knew I couldn't sustain it alone for long, so I decided to set up the company and then find a partner. I also knew I would need to validate the idea. I went out locally and pitched the concept to a few people in an attempt to garner early adopters.

I used the first two major lessons of my personal Venn:

DO WHAT YOU LOVE   **DO WHAT YOU KNOW**

I hit the streets and made sales calls to people with whom I had no personal relationship. The people I spoke with about using our product and services seemed interested, but when things got the slightest bit technical, I lost my audience. They didn't understand the concept. I didn't have a lot of sales materials at the time and would need to create a demo unit. I felt potential customers would have a better understanding of both the concept and the products with a demo unit.

However, even a demo wouldn't have sold the products to the average consumer. After talking and more importantly listening to, a representative sample of potential customers, I learned that the average consumer was not yet ready for an automated home. My product would work much better with commercial users and hobbyists.

For the commercial buyer, our products offered automation, which provided cost savings on energy use. They latched onto the savings benefit. It would be our number one selling point.

For the hobbyist, it was a different sale. The hobbyist was, for the most part, already familiar with the technology and the X-10 products. Hobbyists needed to be sold on uses they had not considered in the past and our superior service.

In the late 1980s, CompuServe was the major player in dial-up bulletin board services (BBS). BBS was the precursor to the internet we know and use today. CompuServe started as a company using spare server resources, selling them to the general public as a dial-up service. CompuServe created a BBS where different areas were available to do everything from messaging to email. They also provided an area to do what I wanted to do—sell products.

I bought the X-10 modules from a corporate distributor at a dealer's wholesale price and resold directly to the consumer at the recommended retail price; basically, a middle, middle-man type organization. I did not have a relationship with the X-10 company itself. I acted as a pass-through agent to sell to the consumer. In fact, I was competing directly with my supplier for customers.

I started the company by selling the HT Systems catalog (home printed and stapled) as well as products through the CompuServe email services and via ads on their BBS.

My home-made catalogs were costly to produce, and the effort to put them together was time-consuming. The catalogs were heavy, since I used standard copy paper stock as opposed to the lighter paper used in professionally printed catalogs, and mailing them was expensive.

I took my idea to the owner of the engineering company where I worked and made a proposal. I would bring HT Systems to his company as a subsidiary and offered him a large ownership share in the company if he joined as a partner. I would run the new company myself while using his resources and funding to grow the company.

He agreed and provided a huge influx of resources and capital to the deal. We started with a plan to make sales locally as a subsidiary to his engineering company. However, we quickly realized that this was not the most practical growth model for the company.

The local market size could not support our growth on its own. The market was just not large enough. The people we visited together didn't have much interest in what we were doing either.

This experience taught me I would not make a success of HT Systems selling products *in* Charleston, South Carolina, but I could if I sold our products *from* Charleston, South Carolina. This distinction is very important and holds true for almost any product. I'm not saying you cannot have a great local company that serves your community at large, but that is far from what I had found for HT Systems. Our products were just too niche.

To create a company with greater reach, I needed platforms and capabilities to make sales. The platform we used was the only one available, and one in which I had experience: CompuServe, and more specifically, the CompuServe Electronic Mall.

The CompuServe Electronic Mall was a basic, text-based service. This service was expensive. We debated the costs and finally gave it a try.

The cost of a "store" in the Electronic Mall was comparable to the standard brick and mortar mall of the time. But there was only an electronic storefront in the Electronic Mall without product pictures, and only text information to support sales and marketing. This text-based mall proved to be less than optimal. Consumers like to see things, even if just in a photo, and the Electronic Mall did not yet offer the posting of photos. The ability to add photos came later and at a premium price. In our case, customers needed more than just a product number, description, and price. They needed ideas, diagrams, and advice.

The idea was interesting; a mall accessible from anywhere. However, the main item we sold in our Electronic Mall store was our catalog, not our products. We sold our catalogs for $5 each, with full credit of the price should the customer purchase a product.

You might wonder why someone would pay for a catalog. Our catalog was popular because it was more than a book of products. It served as a how-to guide with detailed instructions, hints, and tips with ideas for uses. It was more of a handbook with products available for purchase.

We needed to do things differently. We were supposed to be in the business of selling a product, not catalogs. A change in our sales and marketing methods was needed.

There were a few obstacles on our way to success. One was that we required a direct line to the manufacturer, not a distributor. We wanted to *be* the distributor. We also needed to reduce the high cost of shipping our products to consumers. And, we desired to create ways to encourage the hobbyist to become not only a client but a seller of our products as well.

We needed to accomplish several things:

- A larger sales margin
- Lower costs on shipping to consumers
- A method to capture additional sales revenues
- A sales and marketing force to sell our products

I got busy on numerous fronts. I contacted the CEO of X-10 and made a deal. We would get below-wholesale distributer costs, and we would get priority on returns with an extended return window, longer than the standard one year. We would be the company to whom the manufacturer referred consumer inquiries and sales. X-10 would also provide resources to assist with technical issues. We were now a player in the industry with full manufacturer support.

Next, we required a better shipping deal. It was standard in the days before Amazon Prime to pay extremely high shipping rates when buying things via mail-order.

The standard shipping time was more than a week if you paid the lowest price. And it was very expensive to get things shipped next-day or two-day.

I called DHL about shipping services. I arranged a meeting with their commercial sales representative. We were able to make a deal where I could ship up to ten pounds of product for less than five dollars. The rate was perfect. My competitors were charging four to five times that amount for a single item of one pound. At a cost of $4.95 for ten pounds, I could ship boxes with multiple items, charging the client $6.95, and making a profit of over 30 percent on shipping. It was a deal for the consumer and a profit on shipping that my competitors were not seeing.

I then went back to X-10 and negotiated a better deal that added the ability for the consumer to purchase an extended warranty on the products I sold. It was a simple calculation: the consumer could check a box adding 10% to the cost of an item and receive a second year of warranty for that item.

It was a simple, easy to understand, and often-purchased adder. It cost us nothing to provide this extended warranty and almost no one ever used it, so no additional costs were incurred by HT Systems, just a higher profit margin.

Next, I created a program to certify installers (mostly alarm companies or electricians) to both sell and install our products. This provided a network of independent field installers who acted as sales agents for our company.

I obtained one of my first commercial customers through a certified installer. His client was a chain hotel that wanted to reduce electrical costs. We were able to close the sale relatively easily with the use of low-cost modules. We supplied the design expertise to assist the HT Systems certified installer with a successful sale and installation.

The client wanted to control all of the hotel's air conditioning units, allowing the units to be on only when the room was sold and occupied by their customer.

Although the idea itself was simple, the project had its issues. The main issue was a problem with the air conditioning units that occurred intermittently and had no obvious cause. Our installer had purchased the modules, installed, and tested the system successfully.

However, his client complained that some of the room air conditioning units were operating sporadically.

In the hotel business, customer service is one of the most important products sold, and he had some unhappy guests. He wanted the issue fixed and fast. My installer was in over his head, so I loaded up the car and drove to meet him at the hotel site to assess the issue.

This was a day-long drive, but one I was glad I made. I was able to resolve the problem fairly quickly after observing the times of failure and the things that were happening in the hotel when failure occurred. The fix took a few hours, and the client was happy. But to me, it was more important that my installer was equally happy. He went on to sell and install several large projects, more than covering my time and costs for this trip.

The lesson here was customer satisfaction. If you are going to ask someone for their hard-earned money, you are responsible for assuring their satisfaction. I am not suggesting you will always be successful. However, you are responsible for doing everything reasonably within your power to make it happen. My presence at the customer site and assistance with troubleshooting the problem allowed the installer to become more knowledgeable while these actions assured his customer's satisfaction. The customer told his friends in the business, and more sales came as a direct result.

> **"If you are going to ask someone for their hard-earned money, you are responsible for assuring their satisfaction"**

Using some of my lessons from MobiLube, I worked hard to market my products at HT Systems in a better and more illustrative way. At MobiLube, anyone with a car could be our customer. At HT Systems, we had a much more specific and narrowly focused customer audience.

Marketing can be very tricky. For HT Systems, I knew our product was relatively new to most prospective customers and required some skill to implement. I devised a multifaceted way to both find and sell to our potential customers.

Our main sales platform was paper catalogs. I started the design process for our catalog by sitting down on the floor of my home and really thinking about our customers:

- What do they want?
- What do they need?
- What type of person are they?
- What is the skill level required for a successful customer?
- Why would they want our products?

Using these questions, I developed a profile of what our customer would look like, and how much money they would need to earn in their household to be a successful client of HT Systems. This was not a trivial effort.

I then looked at successful mail-order companies. They didn't have to be companies that sold to our potential customers; they just needed to be very successful at what they did.

Some of the catalogs I chose were: Crutchfield, Victoria's Secret, Sharper Image, Sears, and my competitors' catalogs.

I spread all the collected catalogs out on the floor in front of me and looked for similarities. Similarities between an electronics catalog and a women's lingerie catalog. I then asked myself questions:

- What makes a person open this catalog?
- What makes a person buy from this catalog?
- How do I translate this to HT Systems?

What I found was that if you looked closely at any successful catalog business, they were telling a story quickly and simply as to how their products best fit the customer's needs. They made it easy to order and easy to communicate questions back to the company. They included great photos and snappy descriptions.

I took my new found knowledge and worked on creating the best home automation catalog a person would ever receive in the mail. Based on asking myself a lot of questions, one thing that struck me was that a customer needed to know the "how" of our product.

- How is it installed?
- How does it operate?
- How can I use this in my projects?

For the first question, how is it installed, we provided installation instructions and simple wiring diagrams that almost anyone could follow.

Because the products were mostly installed in the home's electrical system by way of replacing light switches and outlets, or the use of a plug-in module, we provided wiring diagrams showing how easy it was to install our products. This took up a lot of valuable real estate in the catalog, but the added value in sales was proven very early.

I answered anticipated questions by creating my own persona within our catalog—a cartoon character known as "Professor Otto Mattic." The Professor appeared throughout the catalog to provide hints, tricks, and tips. It was a way to focus our customers on solutions, and in some cases, show them a problem they might not be aware they had, along with a solution to fix it.

The inclusion of these ideas, even with the extra real estate required to include them, was a game-changer.

People related to the Professor. It was not long after introducing Professor Otto that he started to get fan mail.

My master plan was to close sales by providing information to the customer before the purchase. And it worked.

I was able to track sales cycles using the catalog mailing schedule. I found that the catalog would arrive at the customer's house, and within one to three weeks, the customer would start purchasing products.

Using this data, I could establish a predictive sales cycle and revenues per catalog. Our cost to support all of this activity became my customer acquisition cost.

The challenge was to determine a way to keep the catalog out of the customer's trash can. I needed to keep the catalog on the table, not tossed into the garbage. The longer the customer held the catalog, the more likely a sale, or a repeat sale, would occur.

I determined the base demographics of our client, and I targeted them heavily. The research showed our largest client base was married males. I thought about this fact and realized I had to get by the client's spouse to keep the catalog on the coffee table and out of the trash.

It was more than likely that the buyer's spouse was throwing our rather industrial looking catalog in the garbage. So, I changed the cover. It had to look more like a "House Beautiful" type magazine than an electronics notebook. It had to be of a coffee table quality, and it could not say HT Systems on the cover as the prominent visual element.

So, I changed the catalog to look like a magazine, with a multi-million-dollar home on the cover and gave it an appropriate magazine type name. It worked. The lifetime of the magazine-style catalog increased significantly. This change did have its downside though. In the decision to change the style, I left out the beloved Professor Otto. We still included tips and tricks, but no Professor on the cover or within the catalog. Hate mail arrived shortly thereafter.

Yes, the Professor, although nothing but a figment of my imagination, had become somewhat popular. People didn't like the fact we removed the Professor from the catalog. A few people called and let me know of their displeasure. I also received a couple of letters asking when he would make a return to the publication. Although my intentions were good, time and circumstances dictated that the Professor had met his end. Without pomp and circumstance, the Professor was laid to rest with the final catalog of the old layout.

Not long after we were operating smoothly, the editor of a major magazine approached me. *Home Theater* magazine was expanding and needed a columnist to write about the new automation market and its products. He asked if I would be interested and I agreed to write for them.

I looked at this project as a way to market our company and our products. It provided me with a platform, at no cost, to talk about what we were doing and selling. I just needed to keep the company name and contact info in the reference section of the column, so it didn't appear as a big advertisement.

It worked. Every story had some tie where I could provide a reference at the end to HT Systems. It also led me to write for the home automation magazine, *Electronic House*. Although what I wrote for *Electronic House* was very limited, it was another avenue, along with our ads in the magazine, to raise customer awareness and sales.

We did a lot of interesting and innovative things at HT Systems. One of the most fulfilling was the creation of products. I conceived and engineered a product that our company would go on to sell: an electric water heater controller. The module was an HT Systems exclusive item and was manufactured in our facilities. It allowed for the automated control of a residential water heater, providing for great energy savings.

I installed and tested the first prototype in my home. It reduced electrical usage at the house by over 10%, and the design allowed for a price point with a proven payback of fewer than two years. This alone was something not offered by any other company in the industry.

I also met a software engineer during one of my installer certification classes. He was an educated and talented programmer who was known for writing software utilities which were distributed on floppy discs included in magazines. The discs with his software were in common use throughout the world during the 1980s and early 1990s.

He wanted to collaborate on a home automation software package. I looked at his prototype software, and after seeing how integrated and useful his program was, I agreed to join the project. I would provide user interface oversite and design. He would do all the programming.

Our deal provided him with a license fee for each software package we sold. His abilities, coupled with my design help, allowed for a software package that was easy to sell. At the time, other home automation software was expensive, hard to use, and did not provide a nice user interface. Although functional, the competition's program interfaces were more industrial in design and feel, and the cost of their software was not aligned with an easy purchase decision by the consumer.

I reviewed other popular software and determined we needed a price of less than $100.00. People would buy software under that price point when they did not know how it would look or work. It was a price high enough to provide us with a nice profit and low enough to make the sale. So, we packaged our basic home automation software system at $99.00.

We included extra features in our software upfront and allowed the customer to upgrade, with a fee per feature, after they had installed the software. To accomplish this, we would send the customer a software unlock key when they purchased an upgrade. This key would unlock the additional features.

My software partner and I created approachable software with a reasonable entry price. Compared to the entry-level prices of our competitors' products, which started at $395, we were an easy decision.

EZ Home became the largest selling home-automation package of 1993.

The Abrupt Ending

Life has a habit of getting in the way. Sometimes good, and sometimes bad. It wasn't long after we were running on all cylinders at HT Systems that things once again changed for me, this time for the bad.

Business was performing at a nice cadence. We had a large group of regular customers, and our base was consistently growing. However, I calculated that it would still take several years' worth of steady growth, and the continued evolution of the technology, before home automation would be widely recognized and accepted by the masses.

I felt that home automation would be mainstream by the end of the decade. I was both right and wrong. It became more mainstream, but it took twice the amount of time.

My major life change was the unexpected death of Millie, my wife.

A call came as I stood at a podium, giving certification training in Tampa, Florida. It was the last day of training, and the class had only commenced an hour earlier. The podium had a phone sitting on it that I took little notice of until it rang that morning.

I was in mid-sentence when the phone rang. I looked down at the phone and chuckled. I said, "Hmm, I wonder who that could be," and then picked up the phone. On the other end was a frantic person from my office telling me that my wife was missing.

I stood in shock for a moment and told the person I would call her back. I looked at the class and said, "Let's take a short break while I sort this out."

I left the room, and using the nearest payphone, I called my office back. They told me that there was no information other than a number to call at the police department. I scribbled the number down and immediately called.

I talked to a police detective who informed me Millie was reported missing. It stunned me because nothing like this had happened in the past. I called her office. Millie's manager answered the phone, and informed me she was there, and that she was dead. He told me she had been feeling ill the day before, went to the restroom, and passed away. But no one noticed. It wasn't until they arrived at work in the morning that she was found.

Needless to say, I was in total shock. I took leave of my class and flew back home.

This event thrust me into an unexpected position: I was now a single parent. I needed to change several things in my life immediately. I stopped writing for the magazines and sold my interest in the company. It wasn't the exit I would have wanted, but having two children at home under the age of eight, I made the decision I had to make. There would be time to be an entrepreneur again, but this was not it.

Lessons Learned

I took away some important lessons from my experiences at HT Systems.

The principal takeaway was that the first two lessons of my personal Venn were correct. Doing something I loved and had knowledge of was a big boost to the early success of the company. I could enjoy the work while creating new and interesting things. At HT Systems, we created more than just sales; we created our own products. This was an important goal for me as an engineer.

I also used the power of the pen again writing for the magazines.

My bigger lessons were in the timing of the company. It was becoming an even larger company when I was thrown a curveball with the death of my wife and all the events that followed. However, the company was in a niche market. Hobbyists were the main consumers, and the market was still years, or even decades, away from maturity. In fact, the market is still maturing today.

Had I not exited, hindsight shows it would have taken a lot longer to build the company than I had ever anticipated, simply because of the nature of the products. I have seen some great products introduced and die due to of lack of adoption and use. I have even purchased some of these products for my own home.

Sadly, some of the best products have come and gone. Many of today's products are not designed to a standard that some now-defunct products were, over a decade ago. The reason is the same as it was over twenty-five years ago: home automation is still not mainstream.

So, I added a third circle to my personal Venn:

TIMING IS
EVERYTHING

SIX
Trifecta

A FTER THINGS SETTLED DOWN A LITTLE IN my life, I took a job with a government contractor.

When the company hired me in 1996, they employed me as a senior systems engineer. Although the role they hired me to fill was as an engineer, shortly after my start date, my role was expanded. I was asked to evaluate, and attempt to save, a short-lived foray into a commercial business venture.

Management asked me to look at a new service being started by the company; a commercial business focused on training. The new business unit was being championed by one of the more senior managers. This division would provide Microsoft training and certification for networking engineers. This venture was outside of the company's core competency at the time.

I asked for the business plan so I could assess the idea and see where they were in relation to plan execution. This was the poorest business plan I had ever reviewed. Even worse than MobiLube. Not only did it lack the "plan" part, the document assumed immediate success and profit with an astronomical annual growth rate. The success this plan outlined placed the new business unit well in the black from hour one, day one. It was a ridiculous assumption created by a person who had no experience in commercial business.

I consulted with several people to help me determine what was really going on. I discovered the manager had concocted the idea to save his position—or maybe he believed this plan would be a success. Either way, neither was going to happen. The assumptions were unrealistic; and beyond the lack of realism, the plan placed projected profits in a range that could only be obtained by Microsoft at the time.

After doing some assessment of the industry, I created new projections using realistic scenarios based on research. I then created a new plan for the company that would be doable, depending on their proclivity for losing money. Based on my estimations, there would be losses during a period of well over a year while the division matured, was marketed, and slowly grew to its base potential.

My manager quickly informed me the company could not lose money, period. Therefore, my contingency plan was activated.

The company would return all purchased computers and peripherals to the supplier. If we acted quickly, we could return all equipment without penalty as the supplier offered a free 30-day return guarantee. We would then repurpose the renovations made to the building, turn training rooms into conference rooms and call it a day.

Management accepted my recommendations and quickly acted to reverse the original plan. I was then asked to reach out to businesses for projects to whom I had previously provided automation and controls consulting.

The company wanted to test the waters with a venture into this area of commercial activity. I reached out to one of my contacts at a chemical company and asked to bid on a project. He provided details on a small job. I put a bid package together for the project. It was competitive and accurate. But the wheels of government contracting kicked in. After I submitted the bid package to corporate, others decided to re-work the numbers to the tune of a 300% increase in price. Needless to say, my client contact took one look at our proposed numbers and laughed. I apologized to him and withdrew the bid to prevent personal and corporate embarrassment.

In the following months, I shifted away from the commercial arena and concentrated on various government projects assigned by senior management. Nothing was too difficult, just mundane projects, one after the next—all covering contracts where my experience and expertise added value.

From this point forward, I went about my duties at the company mostly happy but wanting more. I was young and had a lot of energy. I needed to create things, and this experience was not producing creative opportunities for me.

One morning in early September 1997, I received a call from a headhunter. I didn't know a lot about headhunters, but he was asking about a previous associate and wanted a reference. I had worked with his candidate in the past and had provided some supervision of his activities. After I told him about my friend and gave him a glowing recommendation, the headhunter asked me if I was happy in my current position. I told him I was, but his question got me to thinking. Was I really happy? I liked my co-workers, and I even met my future wife there! I liked the company, and I loved where I lived but was I truly happy?

That question stuck in my head for days. A few weeks later, the phone rang again. It was the same headhunter. He told me he had potential projects I may want to consider. This time I was ready for his call. After a bit of soul-searching, I realized I was not happy professionally. Although I was not actively seeking employment, I had decided if an opportunity were to arise which would provide the professional satisfaction I sought, I would take it on. After my focused conversation with the headhunter and the presentation of an offer for a contract meeting my terms, I took the deal.

Later in the week, I submitted my resignation and two-week notice. I was off to Duluth, Minnesota at the start of winter.

Building my Empire

I conceived my new company while on my first independent consulting job in November 1997. I was in Duluth, where it was the beginning of a cold and dark winter. I talked on the phone to an old Navy friend, John Landers. We chatted about the possibility of working together. John and I had met in the early 1980s while we were young sailors in school. We had a lot of talks in those days about someday starting a company together. He wanted to be a corporate pilot, and I wanted to be the CEO.

Looking back, both of the positions we chose further proves the validity of my first Venn circle, "Do What You Love." Today I am a CEO, and John is an avid pilot. When I conceived the company, I named it after both John and myself: Rader-Landers or Raland. However, John decided not to change jobs to join the start-up company, so I went at this on my own.

Raland began with just me as the entire company. Employee number one. I ran the business from a bedroom in my apartment. At first, I would use the company to work as an independent consultant, subcontracting to other companies. This made sense because many contractors with which I was associated, did just that. It was a proven model. I could hang a shingle as a sole proprietor and wait for the jobs to be offered. But I knew even as I started, I needed a lot more.

My project in Duluth was with a company called Lakehead Pipeline. The company transported Canadian oil and liquid natural gas through their pipelines to companies across the United States. I was assigned a project which would increase the flow rates to the end of one of their pipelines, for a client that was expanding and needed more product.

This project led me, for the first time, to Buffalo, New York. I didn't know what to expect in New York State. My only experience in the state had been a trip for my company, HT Systems, to a trade show at the Jacob Javits Center in New York City several years earlier. I knew nothing about Western New York State other than my friend John was from the area and had attended school at the University at Buffalo.

They tasked me with construction management of the new facility and the commissioning process, from land selection to the turnover of a completed oil substation. It was a big job; my first end-to-end project that had a lot of moving parts. Site selection, permitting, contractor oversite, design, engineering, and programming; everything necessary to increase the oil flow rate in a limited time span.

I spent the next nine months traveling back and forth between Duluth and Buffalo. I knew little of the realities of big business and assumed to get the project completed in such a short timeframe there would be "pay-offs" necessary like you see in movies. I was nervous about union issues that could crop up, again like in movies, but to my relief, none of these fears came to pass. I completed the project on time and within budget.

After the contract in Duluth concluded, I accepted a short project just down the road in Minneapolis at a large oil refinery. However, the current economy was all about technology, and the client was selling a commodity, oil. Prices had tanked and were teetering at $10.00 per barrel.

In the oil business, work rises and falls with the price of crude, and the client considered this price catastrophic. All work in the refinery ceased; no expansions or modifications were made to their process, just a slowdown of production and hopes of a quick return of oil prices to at least $15.00 per barrel so layoffs could be reversed, and work could commence.

I was mostly miserable on this project. I had only been on-site for a couple of months as the senior electrical and automation engineer, overseeing a room full of designers and drafters. For the most part, we had been sitting on work, waiting for the budgets to be approved, but with the oil prices fluctuating in a downward direction, there were not a lot of projects green-lighted.

On the last Friday of February 1999, at the end of a miserably slow day, I went home to think about things. I had committed myself personally to assisting the facility, and I wanted to make this project as successful as my project in Buffalo. My nine-year-old son was with me, and I needed to give him a stable environment. So, job shopping was off the table.

I planned to work this project until mid-summer, and if I was still unhappy, I could relocate during summer break and not disrupt another school year for my son. I spent the weekend thinking and planning for this eventuality.

I went to work Monday feeling a little off, and by noon, I knew I had a problem; the flu. It was one of the worst bouts of the flu I had ever encountered. I was horribly sick, running a high fever, and unable to get out of bed. This episode left me out of work for three full days.

Upon my return to the refinery, feeling a little better and free of the fever and body aches, I arrived in my office to see a bunch of little yellow sticky notes on the computer screen. They looked like great news—projects were being green-lighted throughout the facility.

I logged into my computer to find one simple email. It was from the project director, and simply stated: "Bill, when you get in, stop by my office."

I was enthusiastic at work reconvening and quickly stuck my head into the project room to express my excitement to my team. The room that normally housed the 30 designers, drafters, and engineers who worked for me was empty. I brushed off any concern because I had arrived to work a little earlier than normal. I figured no one was in yet.

The director informed me that oil prices had plummeted, and everything was off again. He said my staff had been laid off, and I should take a couple of weeks off myself. He also indicated the oil prices should rebound, and we would start projects again in a month or so after oil prices increased.

For me, this was both an answer and a conclusion. I went back to my desk and wrote a resignation letter – I was out of there. I wanted a lot more stability, and I knew where I would find it. I headed for North Carolina.

I contracted to Bayer Corporation outside of Raleigh. By April, I started to hire employees. Raland had started its long path of growth.

Handing out $10s and $20s

Raland as a corporation officially started with three full-time employees, working in a relatively new aspect of regulatory compliance: computer system validation. All three of us were engineers and had experience with quality systems and more importantly, computers. I even pulled one of my new employees from the project I left in Minneapolis. He was laid off like everyone else and needed work, so I offered him a great job.

We were tasked with ensuring the systems at Bayer Pharmaceuticals were properly documented and validated. Our knowledge of automation systems was superior, and our experience with these systems allowed us to win contracts, beating out our more established competitors.

Being from outside the pharmaceutical industry, we offered a view from a different angle and inherently understood the needs of the client. This, coupled with our work ethic, meant we would ensure a perfect product and meet the timelines. Our hard work quickly captured the respect of our clients and the envy of our competitors.

During this time, I recognized that in order to have a sustainable company, I had to grow outside of Bayer and quickly. I watched what the competition was doing. I noted their main marketing strategy, inside the client, consisted of company branded t-shirts.

My competitors would sell their company-logoed shirts to employees and anyone else who would purchase them. Their penetration was pathetic because no one wanted to pay to advertise.

Realizing this, I tried a different approach. I produced shirts and hats to give away at no charge. I gave them to anyone who asked, for free. All associates had an ample supply of shirts. Nice shirts. Polos, not t-shirts. I gave them away at every meeting with a new or prospective client; I handed a shirt and hat to them as a "Thank you for your time."

It was a good marketing strategy when meeting prospective clients. It helped to grow customer acquisition, and the overall branding cost was minimal. I asked everyone who worked for the company to hand out the free shirts and hats sparingly, concentrating primarily on those who could provide projects. I even handed out our shirts to competitor's employees—who doesn't love a high quality, free shirt? I found most everyone did, and my company name was everywhere.

However, the plan almost backfired. I arrived in a large meeting room to discuss a project. The client was there, along with a few competitors working on different aspects of the project. I looked around at a sea of black shirts with the Raland logo emblazoned across the left breast of nearly everyone in the room. It was a disconcerting yet fulfilling sight.

One of the competing companies noted this "sea of black" and placed a complaint with the client. The funny thing was, all of his employees were wearing my shirts, yet I wasn't.

I never stopped handing out the free "swag" even as we grew. It is important to get your company name as recognized as possible and establish a constant presence, so there is familiarity with your brand. This is the exact tactic used by large companies using standard advertising venues.

Even if someone has no experience with your company, brand recognition creates a familiarity that can be advantageous to your business.

The key to my branding was to make our logo look familiar and friendly. I made the name short, and the logo simple. These two things together created a familiar "ring" to our otherwise unique name and logo. I kept the color pallet simple and the logo uncluttered—basically, a red triangle with a six-letter name.

"Familiarity is the first step in the process of developing trust"

I recall in the early days of Raland a person saw our logo and instantly said he knew us, and we had a "great" reputation in the industry. This was flattering but not possible. We had only existed a few months, and at that time, no one knew us. We had yet to build any type of reputation.

That simple design and friendly-looking logo were all it took, and the person felt he was familiar with us when he could not possibly have been.

Often in business, I see clever spellings or created words in a business name that do not breed a sense of familiarity. This can sometimes work, like a business introducing a new product, but in the service industry, you want to create trust.

To get trust, start by using familiarity. People like to do business with and purchase products from companies with which they feel safe. If they are shopping for a service, they want to know they can trust your company to solve their issues. Familiarity is the first step in the process of developing trust.

Obviously, trust is best obtained through experience. But with a new company, you must use a little psychology to get in the door.

After that, you can earn their trust by doing an outstanding job, just like we did at Raland.

We were in the business of solving problems. Our clients had real issues, and we were there to make the client look good. Our official company tagline was "quality people providing quality solutions," but my personal motto was "make the client look good, and we will all win."

During the 1990s, it was relatively unheard of to operate a company virtually. I ran into several issues winning clients when they asked about our offices and internal operations. The clients often felt if they did business with a company that operated virtually and something went wrong, it could leave them holding the bag. To them, virtual meant we would just disappear into the night. This was not an easy preconception to overcome.

When I was attempting to win larger projects where the clients had the most exposure, they wanted a service company with an office. The clients held back projects we could easily have accomplished and even save them money—due to this fear.

Because of the frustration created by this attitude towards our virtual operations, in early 2004, I shifted our business model slightly with the addition of two physical office locations. Even with the offices, we were able to keep our overhead at an astonishingly low percentage of overall operational costs.

Adding a physical presence to the company was an idea met with enthusiasm by our clients. To celebrate the move of our headquarters to the 34th floor of the Chase Tower in downtown Indianapolis, I held a grand holiday party in December 2004. We pulled out all the stops for this party. It would make a splash, showing we were a major player in the industry. I invited clients, associates, and friends. In the past, I had run things quietly, but this was about to change. This coming-out party also pushed me into the limelight as the leader of the company.

Early Lessons Taken Forward

In previous years, I had held everything close to the chest. I operated in the near shadows, so as not to stick out too much. In the past, being too vocal and taking leadership roles at customer sites caused me some issues with competing companies. My intentions were good in these situations, but my competition saw me as a threat and did everything in their power to remove my company and me from the picture.

When working with one of our first clients, our competition was in a position of power. Their president, after seeing my company and its highly skilled and qualified people arrive, went into a panic mode. Our competing company's president was always on-site and had the client's ear. He made up stories about me personally and asked he be placed "in charge" of me while I was on site.

Not knowing the actual story, the client agreed and allowed him to move me from working with my team to working for him directly. It was a great move on his part. He could watch my every contact with the client and attempt to intervene anytime the client asked my team for assistance.

He believed he could set me up for a fall using his limited focus of control. However, he made a major misstep. He made his plans to oust me known to a few others, including one of the client managers. This manager warned me to "watch out" for the competitor, that he had a scheme to remove Raland from the project. His attempt was put into play a few weeks later when my guard was down. He asked that I go offsite to meet with the client at one of the customers' other facilities.

I interpreted the request as just another project and went to the meeting. The location was a 45-minute drive from the main facility where we were assigned. I arrived on time and entered the building. I looked around and found there was no sign-in sheet, a standard protocol for entering a secured building. This was not completely uncommon for this client, so I didn't think twice about it. I looked for the person with whom I was to meet, and they were not there. After trying to call my contact with no success, I went back to the main facility.

The overall trip took about two hours. My "manager" had set his trap; I was a pawn in his game.

After I submitted the chargeable time for the week, he went into full search and destroy mode. He went to the client, who had gone along with his demand to manage me, and told her I had falsified time charges. This, of course, was a complete and utter fabrication, but his plan was actually quite brilliant. He knew there was no way I could prove anything because there was no one to corroborate my side of the story. In fact, I was not even given the opportunity to prove my whereabouts.

He then demanded that my company and I be removed from the project. He offered to bring in the needed people to cover for losing my team.

He pulled me aside and let me know that it was check and mate. I sat listening to him, realizing he had only won a battle, not the war. Sure, he had won a competition I really didn't consider I was in. Even the client questioned his actions. He obviously was not one to place integrity before profit.

He was successful in removing me from *his* project, but he didn't do any major damage to Raland. The client had only agreed that he could be in charge of me. She further stated that the maneuver was a big mistake on his part but allowed him to remove only me from the one project I was working on under his charge.

She did not allow him any other leeway, including his attempt to remove my team and me from the corporate site. I still had an office on-site, and the Raland team was intact. His nefarious scheme was only partially successful, but the attempt left a real burn for me and my trust level plummeted.

After this episode, I considered any competition to be hostile. I would always make sure I could not be lulled into believing that something like this would not happen again.

I withdrew and no longer considered competing companies to be team members when working together. In my earlier days as an entrepreneur, I believed people until they proved otherwise. I no longer give trust away that easily. I require that people earn it. The other person's motivation is now a consideration in all my activities.

My trusting nature caused Raland some difficulty, but it was not as disastrous an ending as the competition had planned. I learned my lesson.

Raland went on to outlast the competition at that site and create not only great jobs, but the experience brought me lifetime friendships with several of the client managers.

Raland's Coming of Age

The holiday party in the Chase Tower was "My Party." I was in control. I even invited a few of our competitors just to show them I may have been quiet in the past, but that time was over. Get on board with me, or move the hell out of my way.

The tactic worked. Clients and competitors alike called me—clients with offers of work and competitors with offers of collaboration. I took the work from the clients and as for the competitor's offers; I might work with them, but at an arm's length and under my terms.

This method served us well for years, and we had very steady growth.

However steady it was, by mid-2005 I felt that our growth was too slow. I wanted to grow at a much faster pace.

The Power of M&A

As I pondered our growth rate, I began to focus on an idea. I thought about the power of two or three versus the power of one. I thought one way to grow Raland might be through bringing in the power of another company through merger or acquisition (also known as M&A). This could provide for a bump in growth if done right.

I took the next couple of years, clearly identifying my goals for a merger and then identifying potential partners from the industry we served.

During this period of company and personal growth, I learned a great deal. My experiences in M&A are reflected in this popular *Forbes* story I wrote in May 2017:

Forbes—May 2017:
7 Ideas to Make Your Merger or
Acquisition A Success

During my many years in business, I have completed five mergers and one acquisition, and sold four companies. Each transaction was examined closely and always thought to be in the best interest of both the company and those who had ownership stakes in the business.

History shows that after the party is over, and the hard work begins, things rarely turn out as anticipated.

I could write a book on each merger and acquisition (M&A) in which I have been involved. None ever resulted as planned. In hindsight, I can attribute the majority of issues to being a small company with multiple, mostly-equal, owners.

Each M&A started good, had a transition period with issues and uncertainty, and in the end, resulted in a better company. It was always the "transition" period that was the most challenging and resulted in the greatest cost on multiple levels.

So, you want to buy a company or expand your current company? Here are some ideas to reduce your pain:

1. If you are thinking of a merger, get to know your potential partners. You want and need to know the person and their

company from the inside out. Don't jump into things without fully vetting the individuals. When I say fully vetting, I mean fully. Do background checks. Require references and talk to all of the references. Talk to the prospective partner's employees. The attitude of the employees will provide a much clearer picture of the company and the individual as a leader.

2. Talk to the prospective partner's customers or current clients, as well as those that have left, and find out why. Read customer reviews and learn as much as you can about the future viability of the company based on what people say. Customers can tell a lot about the company. Their happiness, or displeasure, is a sure sign of how the company and its leadership perform.

3. Look at the prospective partner's books, and then have your financial experts do the same. Go back at least five years, and for good measure, seven. Look for abnormalities, little ones that are repeated. Does the potential partner have problems keeping the books straight or do the books show inconsistencies? If so, you might want to rethink your merger—this could be indicative of deeper issues.

4. Are there or have there been issues with state or federal tax authorities? This could signal potential issues in the future. Look at all documents relating to past tax issues and ensure that they are fully resolved.

5. Do a deep dive on their operations. What do the employee files look like? Do they have operational procedures in place? Do the employees know these procedures and if so, do they follow them? Having current, fully vetted procedures and policies can save a lot of pain.

6. The most successful merger or acquisition has full buy-in from all parties. This includes not only the owners and stockholders, but the employees and customers. All parties need to understand the vision of the merged companies and see the upside. They have to understand why a merger is necessary or desirable and in their best interest.

7. It is of utmost importance to merge the team of employees first and foremost. I have seen cases where the employees are not in line with the company mission years later, and this is a very bad thing.

Transitioning can be hard. I have found time and time again that people generally hate change.

They like their coffee a certain way, and they feel the same way about their company operations. In a merger, the employees are key to the success, more so than the owners or senior management. However, it takes the senior management's leadership to successfully implement the merger.

It's less about the day you pop the corks and celebrate, and more about next month and next year. Never underestimate the amount of time that will be required in absorbing a company or changing the way things operate to "your way" or to a successful melding of the best of both companies.

Recognize areas that are operating well and allow them to continue. I am sure there are a lot of things working, or you wouldn't have considered a merger or acquisition in the first place.

I have seen people take a well-oiled machine and "clog the cogs" by ignoring what works well and doing a wholesale change to "their way".

Even if you desire to change operations, take your time. Some things need immediate alterations and others can wait. Work on the bottom line first. Ensure that the employees and customers are taken care of and happy, then work to adjust the operations to support the goals of the new management.

One company I assisted had two rival factions working against the goals of the merged corporation as they had an "old guys" vs. "new guys" attitude. It took the removal of many of the "old guys" to correct the roadblocks and arrive at a fully operational business.

Lastly (and most importantly), trust your gut reaction to everything you see during an M&A. If things don't feel right, they probably are not. Approach every merger or acquisition with caution and an inquisitive mind. If you have a bad gut feeling it might be best to delay or abandon the merger or acquisition.

* * *

My original title for this *Forbes* article was "Success and Failure With Mergers and Acquisitions." However, I focused the article on the ways to attain success.

I could write a separate book on each merger and acquisition with which I have been involved. The difficulties of getting tangled with others in business cannot be overstated. I guarantee there will be challenges; I have first-hand experience and the scars to prove it.

The Start of M&A for Raland

By the second half of 2008, the United States was experiencing one of the most difficult economies since the Great Depression; however, Raland had performed quite well. The difficult economic times for the country had been a time of great growth opportunity for us. We entered this period with low overhead, a result of my commitment to operating as a virtual company from conception. The company was growing, but still not at the pace I had desired.

In mid-2008, I had taken a shot at growth through a merger. I vetted several companies but realized that I needed more than just "a company" for a solid merger. I needed a partner.

The process began a couple of years earlier. I was approached by a person on a project site in Pennsylvania. He had a small consulting company and proposed the idea of working together. But it didn't happen at the time because shortly after his proposal, he took a full-time position as an executive with a company where we both were contracting.

I watched him for over a year as he navigated the inner workings of a rapidly growing biotechnology company. We would meet for dinner and discuss current business and future plans. I felt good about him overall, so when I discovered the biotech company he was working for was in the process of being acquired, I made a proposal to him.

With the sale of his employer to a larger entity, he was more than likely going to be deemed redundant—which in layman's terms means he knew he would lose his job within a set period after the company was acquired. He was starting to plan his next move, which was going back to his small consulting company. His company had been operated by others while he was employed at the biotech but had limited growth because he was the main business development resource.

We agreed to meet in late 2007 for dinner near my office in Indianapolis. At dinner, we shared our desires and ideas. We walked away with a gentleman's agreement to combine our efforts, his company into Raland Technologies, and to co-manage our new company for growth.

Our merger took place in early 2008, and we hit the ground at full speed. We quickly took an ever-increasing market share and expanded our reach. Our work was rewarded greatly. We won nearly every project we bid and had great financial returns. We built a solid war chest of cash, providing us the resources to start looking towards new acquisitions and mergers during the down economic cycle. We planned to bail out failing enterprises who had promise and fit our business model. We then would build a larger and stronger company with a planned exit within seven years. This placed us with a planned exit near the end of 2015.

I was called the "idea guy" and was given the job of "dreaming" and the title of Chief Business Development Officer and President of Research and Development. I was to sit in my office and think up new ideas and plans. I took this job seriously. For me, it was the position I was made for: I was, and am, an idea guy, and the merger allowed me great latitude to dream up new things.

Within Raland we created the "Kapow Idea Factory." It was named after what my wife Pat called my *"Kapow"* ideas (my old Eureka! moments). I have always been a problem solver, and the opportunity to focus on potential new initiatives was freeing, and fun. I started to document ideas and execute on those that had some sort of promise. My role also required me to review new M&A opportunities.

My first goal was to expand the communications division within Raland into a larger, more formidable offering. We had success in this area already. We would obtain training projects and sub-contract much of the creative work while keeping the instructional design in-house. Pat was originally tasked with building the division starting in 2006 and had won major projects and industry awards over 24 months.

I planned to acquire the company where we had been sub-contracting our development work for this division. The company itself seemed solid: 20-plus years in operation and an outward appearance of stability and solid management.

The company had performed so well for us, and for Pat in her time previous to Raland. They seemed the best fit and the strongest candidate for us. In fact, we didn't even look at other options. My partner and I spent time together with the management of the target company and visited their facilities to meet the team.

Internally we huddled to determine an offer price but ended up letting our acquisition target set the price, as it was substantially lower than we had identified as our ceiling price. In fact, at the time I felt a bit guilty accepting the number.

However, before finalizing the acquisition of the training company, I had another target company to visit. My partner suggested that we look at the potential to purchase a small clinical research lab in Boston. I traveled to Boston to talk to the management of the lab and to tour their facility.

The labs and offices were beautiful. The equipment was new, and the facility was in top condition. I conducted a short review of their quality system and many of their operational procedures. This place was incredible. The attention to detail and the condition of the property were exceptional. But there was an issue. It was mid-week, and the facility was a virtual ghost town. No one was working. There was not even a receptionist in place to greet me when I arrived.

I sat in their conference room after the facility tour and procedure review. Besides me, their CFO and CEO were the only people present for the meeting. The CEO was an exceptional Ph.D. however, not much of a business-person. She had leveraged all of her personal assets to build this incredible facility but didn't have any business pipeline to speak of. She had some small customers who were her personal friends and associates, but the financial burn rate of the operation far outpaced her receivables. At their rate of cash burn, she would be bankrupt by year-end, and there were no booked sales in-house to lower the burn rate or extend this endpoint.

The CFO and CEO were honest and open in our conversations, but even then, I thought they were probably off on the numbers presented. I estimated they were likely 20% worse off than disclosed, either by intent or ignorance. It would only take a weekend to do a full financial review of the company. Although we could have acquired the operation for near-zero up-front out-of-pocket cost, the purchase would have cost upwards of one million dollars more than originally anticipated over the first six months to generate enough free cash flow to cover their base expenses. This would have put us in a position of needing a perfect run for the following year to come out of this deal, and our training company deal at a net positive.

Any further downturn in the economy would put us in the same position these companies were in, and this was not what we were trying to accomplish.

I decided making the lab acquisition successful would take most of our reserve capital and recommended against this opportunity. We were most interested in expanding our opportunities within existing clients, so the least risky position was to purchase the training company and pass on the lab.

The training company acquisition increased our footprint, and our overhead, significantly. Our due diligence with this company was light. We had been working with them for a couple of years, knew the team, and had experienced their professionalism and high-quality work output. So, we proceeded with the acquisition based on the merits of their product.

We did not take a deep dive into their financials and sales projections. I have found that this is a common mistake when you have a good working relationship with a vendor - you trust everything is good.

If their previous year was a great year, and the last three quarters show good financials, this can tell some of their story. But not their full story. Always ask for projections, and then follow-up with direct conversations with their clients about future work.

I have been subjected to many surprises in M&A. After the agreements are signed, you may well learn that the large contracts claimed are bogus, or there are other major issues financially or operationally. The phrase "trust but verify" was created for these types of situations. Transitioning can be hard. I have found time and time again that people generally hate change, and the nature of M&A is change.

I've broken my experiences with M&As down into three short case studies:

Study number 1: The fire sale

One of my M&As was at the height of the great recession. My company was very strong financially, while many other companies were struggling. We were looking for potential acquisitions in our space to grow both our customer base and our offerings.

I traveled around looking at companies, some extremely tempting targets; however, we settled on a company that was in distress and whose core business would allow us to expand our services.

We looked at the financials which the target's management provided, and realizing they were in extreme trouble, asked to look at their client list and open projects. On the surface, things looked promising. Our target looked to have an under-capitalization issue.

The company had factored receivables and maintained poor margins, but with the application of proper project management and the renegotiation of a few contracts, we could turn the situation around quickly. The main incentive we had was their assurance that they were the winner of a large government contract worth millions of dollars which would pay out over the next couple of years.

We planned to buy out the debt of the company, and restructure its operations, taking advantage of our infrastructure, which would reduce overhead and increase margins.

In theory, our solution, coupled with the promised booked sales, would yield a fantastic return. In reality, we found the contracts presented as booked business (including the large government contract) were nothing more than potentials. I trusted my partner had completed due diligence in this effort, and I was promised all they showed me was factual. As it happened, this was not accurate.

During initial reviews, I suggested we let the target company fail because of its debt load before we came in. However, the partner who discovered the target and who was pushing the acquisition was not in favor of this plan. He cited the large government contract as the compelling reason for the immediate bailout of the target. He said we would lose the government contract if we did things my way.

I agreed to the purchase.

I made a huge mistake. I trusted the word and presentation of a distressed individual and a partner who was looking for a personal win. The misrepresentation was something I could have considered actionable due to the fraudulent claims. However, resorting to legal action would have cost substantially more than fixing the issues in-house. The answer existed in executing a new plan which would salvage the acquired company and reorganize the newly gained division to enable sustainable growth.

Although the result was not as anticipated upfront, we could turn the business around. However, we incurred a much higher cost than was initially expected from both a financial and a personal standpoint.

The partner who had spearheaded and pushed for the purchase resigned from our company. I took over and moved to line the merged company into our operations and profit model. It took well over two years to turn the acquisition from a fiasco into a solid operational division producing a net positive return. Overall, we ended up investing a lot of time and money to salvage this business when we were promised a massive profit opportunity less than six months after acquisition.

Lesson learned: if it sounds too good to be true, do a deeper dive, and take more time. The best-case scenario in our situation would have been the target company going out of business before our acquisition. If this had occurred, we could have bought their assets at a much lower cost, and their liabilities would have been dealt with by the target closing its operations prior to our purchase. This scenario would have been much better for our company, even if it came at the risk of losing existing and potential clients.

Buyer beware.

Study number 2: Poor due diligence

The key to a good merger is to treat it as an acquisition. In this case, we acquired the vast majority of an existing company. We then planned for a nice merger with everyone on board with our plan. I spent a couple of months working to create anticipation and excitement about the merger. I saw the addition of new people and skills as a huge benefit to our existing clients. The merger went beautifully on the surface. All plans came together in an orderly fashion.

After the merger papers were signed, problems came to the surface quickly. Following the merger, sales by the division were horrible. So much so that costs associated with the acquisition far outstripped income from the division.

Our due diligence relied on the projections provided by the acquired company's management, and the sales projections were much rosier than the facts. Had we had completed a deeper dive into the sales cycle of the company during our review phase we would have easily found the cycle was directly affected by the economic situations at a couple of their key clients, and the clients were essentially dying because of technology shifts. It was like buying a buggy whip company at the dawn of the automobile era—not a lot of growth potential, let alone a guarantee of profit.

The solution was obvious, and the reason we had originally targeted the company for purchase. I wanted to bring this company into our industry. Their abilities and technology were great assets. The team had all that was needed to allow expansion in the life science industry, where we already had a firm footing.

To expand into our market space, the acquired staff needed to learn a new concept and processes specific to our industry. They had already gained exposure to our clients while acting as a subcontractor to our company, but now we would challenge them to become experts.

Through much of the merger process, I had been fairly ill and had issues with my medical treatment. At the time of the merger, I asked my original partner to act as the outwardly facing CEO of our company. We would operate as partners but have a typical corporate structure to the outside world.

Some in the company were less aligned with the company mission. As a result, our new CEO thought we should let the acquired company operate as it had in the past.

The issue was the acquired company was not operating in a method which would result in the best financial outcome. It was plagued with inefficiencies, and in some cases, outright refusal to follow the direction of the new management.

This situation resulted in employees that were not aligned to the company's core values, and unsure of who they reported to each day.

This is an example of poor communication and management not aligned in vision.

Lesson learned: communicate clearly and create vision alignment with management. If you must step aside and let a partner assume the helm, be sure you are on the same page. This comes through proper communication of your vision and follow-up to ensure things are running according to your company mission.

Study number 3: Golden Merger

Here, both parties agreed on every aspect of the merger. This scenario is not common, but it should be expected. In this case, our vision was in sync from the beginning. It is important to have the same goals when merging.

During discovery and negotiation, we met regularly. We got to know each other and shared a similar passion and vision. We planned all aspects of the merger meticulously, and everyone had a purpose and responsibility. We managed a low-cost merger, a fair equity split, and a low-stress action.

This did not happen by accident. Prior to the merger, I had a business relationship with my future partner. I spent time getting to know him and his abilities. Due diligence was thorough and complete.

No items were missed, and plans were laid out and agreed to up front.

We executed the business merger and operation changes cleanly and steadily. The company grew quickly with happy, repeat customers, and equally happy associates.

Lesson Learned: In any merger or acquisition, take the time to look at everything. Talk to people: customers, employees. The only way you really find out who a person is, is by taking the time to get to know them. It is said that a merger was like a marriage, and this is very true. Take the time to date before you jump into things.

Conclusion: Keep it simple.

The best advice I can provide as a seasoned M&A entrepreneur is to treat every merger as an acquisition. There must be one company that takes over the other, and the dominant company should manage the merged entity. Holdovers in executive management must be few and either reassigned or let go. In my experience, holdovers send the wrong message of how things will be run after the merger and could lead to more problems and expense than one might ever imagine.

Keep it simple. The top company's name is the marquee name—no hyphenated or combined names. It creates confusion among both employees and clients.

With any merger or acquisition, leaders must think about employee retention. I wrote a story in *Forbes* about this in August 2017:

Forbes—August 2017
How To Maximize Employee Retention

Everyone wants a job until they have it. And then, most are looking for their next position. It's a cold hard fact. Even if you think your employees are happy and stable, think again. Over and over again, I have had great, loyal, happy employees hand me their notice. It has never been about the job they have, or issues with the company. I know this as a fact, as in most cases, I have stayed in touch with my former employees in their follow-on endeavors.

Why do they jump ship?

They jumped because the next opportunity gave them a new and perceived greener pasture. Most found this was more of a fantasy than a fact, but all wanted the golden ring. Essentially, they were all "self-promoting." This is where a person decides that they need to move to a new company to advance in their profession. Sometimes this can be true and depending on the size and growth of your business, this may be a fact for most if not all of your employees at some point.

How do you keep them?

Just how you keep your employees is a question for you, your accountant, and your tax advisor. Often, it is not money that causes the employee to jump to a new company. It is the new job position and/or level of authority. It is basically their desire to climb the ladder.One way to fix the issue of employee churn, or at least extend the time an employee commits to your organization, might be to create an Employee Stock Ownership Plan, or ESOP. An ESOP allows you to grant an interest in your company based on employee commitment.

An ESOP requires you, as an owner, to give up some portion of your ownership in the company. It can be created in ways that encourage both employee longevity but also production. Longevity as the employee vests into an ESOP, and production because the better the company performs, the more value the employees create for themselves.

Engage your employees.

As a leader, you should always engage your employees. Listen to and act on their ideas and issues. The worker of today wants to be part of the company's process and success, and holding on to them, especially the top performers, is not going to be easy. What I have always tried to do was to create an environment where the associate felt that their efforts were not only appreciated, but also truly valued.

There are a number of ways to accomplish this, everything from employee-of-the-month type awards to cash bonus awards for performance. Be creative based on your employee base and industry. But always, engage the employees. You might even set up some sort of idea contest, where they tell you how you might improve engagement in, and commitment to, your company.

Keep in mind that employees today do not invest as much time to a company than they have in past decades. We are in a different decade. No longer do people commit their working lifetime to a single company. The millennial employee is adventurous and wants to make a difference, in a much different fashion than in the past. Employees want more than a job. They want purpose.

Help them along their path.

Don't take it personally when the guy you never thought would leave, does just that. When they come to you and share their intention to leave, make it easy. Help them. Give them ideas and advice. Allow them to help you with their transition. They can and will become a sales and recruitment division—outside your company, helping you in your mission. I have had former employees provide projects, new employee recommendations and much more.

If you value your former employee like your newest hire, it becomes a win-win situation.

***

Lessons Learned

My trifecta company benefitted from the hard lessons I learned on my journey to that point, and I enjoyed the success of Raland. However, my experience in empire building brought with it many additional lessons. I think the most important one was - Don't forget the lessons you learned early in your career (or life). Apply these lessons. Initiating and growing Raland also provided me with many additional lessons:

- **Branding and marketing** only work if you target your branding message and have a goal.

- **A recognizable brand = familiarity; and familiarity = trust.** People are always more likely to trust the things they are most comfortable with; therefore, make your brand clean, clear, and familiar.

- **It's great to trust people, but competition is defined as rivalry for supremacy.** Never forget that fact!

- **Always run the numbers.** Sometimes the truth lies deep inside the numbers. Even if the whole picture is presented and looks good on the surface, issues can be in the business cycle, the client pipeline, or other areas. These items can show good numbers today but spell problems after a merger or acquisition.

- **Do the due diligence** to the point of overdoing it. Even if it takes longer than anyone desires.

- **When you merge with a company, you are actually either buying their company or selling yours.** The larger or acquiring company must prevail in all areas for smooth operations moving forward.

- **Planning is crucial.** Keep it simple, cut over in an organized fashion, and operate as one identity for success.

SEVEN
The Diagnosis

HORTLY BEFORE ONE OF MY MERGERS, I received a life-altering diagnosis.

I had an issue in early 2002 with pain and stiffness in my legs and loss of balance when walking in the dark. I was subjected to many tests that resulted in several unanswered questions. I was referred to a neurologist who quickly diagnosed me with Guillain-Barré Syndrome (GBS), a disorder in which the body's immune system attacks part of the central nervous system.

After receiving a series of powerful drug infusions, I was told everything was fixed, more-or-less, and the chance of the issue reoccurring again was less than five percent. The physician proclaimed me a poster child for success in the treatment of this disease. He said that at least I didn't have Multiple Sclerosis (MS) as that would have been "really bad."

I continued to have recurring issues with pain when I attempted to go for a run, something I did often before my issues with GBS. I also experienced fatigue and a strange turning in or curling of the palm of my right hand. But to me, this was just the left-over effects of GBS, and I did not seek additional medical consultation. I continued to build my company but would no longer go for a nice stress-relieving run in the evening.

With any neurologic condition, or even for life in general, stress has a negative impact. And to put it lightly, running a services company is very stressful. In fact, most of my life, I have submitted myself to constant stress. From my first company through today, I have constantly placed myself into stressful situations. I always felt I thrived on the challenge, and that the pressure of the situation was merely a necessary evil associated with the advancement of a cause.

I remember as a youth having a small rash break out on my lower left arm when I was under the stresses of Aquatic Diving Company. It wasn't constant, but as situational pressure was applied, it manifested in a physiological response. A friend's mother noted this and suggested that the stress was a bit much for a kid my age. She suggested I do something to reduce my anxiety. I shook off her suggestion of seeking medical advice about my problem and went about my business.

At this time in my life, I had a great pressure relief valve. If I felt stressed, I jumped into my boat and went to sea.

I left behind the day's burdens and floated with engines in idle, along the shore of my home on the Gulf of Mexico. It was the seagulls and me. Quiet, peaceful, and beautiful. I only needed to go to sea for a few hours to be entirely rejuvenated and ready to face the world again.

However, my most peaceful location was underwater. I would don my diving gear, roll off the side of the boat and float quietly, 30 feet underwater. Nothing but the warm water of the Gulf, near absolute silence. Nothing but me and my thoughts. Absolute peace.

This was long ago and not something I did anymore. I shifted to running while in the Navy. But now, the issues from what I thought had been GBS prevented that outlet. Life was way too busy with little time available for me. I no longer had a relief valve.

Prior to the GBS diagnosis, I was having an issue similar to when I was younger. This time I was older and a little wiser; I sought a physician's opinion. He did an exam and determined that I was secreting a large amount of histamine. He said this caused my skin irritation. He told me to reduce the stress in my life, and I would get better. Although decades later, his advice was exactly the same as my friend's mother.

In September 2009, the GBS was back, or so I thought. I had the same symptoms with the addition of a weird new problem—my eyes occasionally "twittered" rapidly back and forth. It only happened a couple of times, so I dismissed it as a strange muscle issue. Not an uncommon reaction to a small yet noticeable event.

At the time, I was living in the Washington DC area growing Raland. I wanted the best the area had to offer, so I located a physician affiliated with Johns Hopkins Hospital. I saw a local neurologist who not only called my physician from seven years earlier but conducted his own tests. Several of them. He repeated the tests completed by the initial physician and added more.

The day the results were in, Pat and I sat in his office. The physician told me that without a doubt, I was never afflicted with GBS. I was happy to hear this news, but then quickly realized he was about to tell me something my wife and I seriously did not want to hear. I felt numb as we listened to his next words:

"Bill, you have Multiple Sclerosis."

He let me breathe a little and ask a few questions, but in a situation like this, there is little you can think of outside of the echo of the words you just heard.

All I could hear for a few moments was a ringing in my ears, *"you have MS, you have MS."*

I thought, "Did I hear him right? The last guy said I had GBS... What does this mean?"

He wanted to start treating me with very high-dose steroids and was ready to set the process up immediately.

I sat for a few minutes thinking quietly, asked a question or two, and then set an appointment to return and discuss further treatment options a few days later.

It was the type of diagnosis no one wants to hear. It says, "Gee, we found an issue we're not entirely sure what to do about. Everyone is different, but we can offer a few very expensive, painful, and life-altering treatments that statistically can help reduce issues for approximately 35% of the patient population..."

Pat and I sat in the car outside the doctor's office for a few moments gathering our thoughts. I am sure her head was spinning as much as my own. We had only been married for three years. Now, not only did I face a lifetime of issues, but by default, she did as well. I said the only thing which seemed right at the time: she could, without fault or issue, leave our marriage because she didn't sign up for this.

I quickly found out this was the wrong thing to say.

We drove quietly back to our house in Frederick, Maryland.

The next morning, a delivery person knocked on our front door with a big box. He said, "You need to open this. Some items must be refrigerated at once."

I opened the box, and there was a bunch of medical supplies and a three-ring binder of instructions. The directions stated that I was to "self-infuse," which meant I would be connecting myself to a variety of medications, infusing them directly into my veins. And, if there was an issue, I should call a number that was listed in the binder.

I was initially horrified but then realized a home care nurse would come out and insert the catheter into my vein. This was good because although I had worked for a long time in the pharmaceutical industry, it's a huge leap to think I could insert a catheter into my own vein—kind of like expecting an airline baggage handler to pilot a plane—not the same job description.

I self-infused the harsh chemicals for three days. At the end of this period, they told me I could just "pull the catheter out myself." I was hardly ready for that, so I called upon Pat to do the duty.

Now understand that she is not a nurse. Not even close. Neither Pat nor I had any notion of how to properly remove the needle, so a job that would take a professional a fraction of a second took us a good minute.

As she started to extract the needle slowly, I looked in the opposite direction and placed my thoughts elsewhere. She gasped at the whole concept of doing "medical" work. She feared hurting me, much as anyone in her position would.

It was during this activity that I experienced what I have only heard people talk about. We were sitting at the kitchen table, removing the catheter when a moment of inspiration hit me; a better way to do infusions.

I grabbed a napkin and started to sketch. Pat was carefully working to remove the needle from my left hand, and I was using my right hand to sketch out what would become my invention, "RxFusion." This epiphany also started a process that would take full shape about one year later.

Over the next year, I not only had a flair of the MS, but I also had a reaction to a prescribed medication that required an emergency room visit. All the while, I was being pressured by a partner to approve an acquisition. To say the least, 2010 was a year of pain on more than one front.

Partner Pain

Partners can be an interesting bunch: if you pick the right ones, things will be great! And if you have the misfortune of selecting the wrong ones, you will pay a price.

A rule I have adopted because of the many issues I have encountered: Think long and hard before taking on a partner. Even though I always entered into partnerships with the goal of harmony and success, the two hardly ever coexisted.

Key items to consider before considering partnering:

- What are your goals from a partnership?
- Do you really know your potential partner's goals and ambitions?
- What is *their* motivation for partnering with *you*?
- Have you ever worked with this person?
- How does your potential partner handle stressful situations?
- Would you be willing to hand them all your personal financial information and bank pins for a year while you were out of the country?

No matter how well you think you know your partners or how well you think you vetted them, unless you start a business the same day and time with the partner, I would advise proceeding carefully or not at all. And if you proceed, make sure you have a written Partner Plan agreed to and drawn up by professionals, which outlines the nature and method of the partnership.

"Think long and hard before taking on a partner"

My experience as a submariner taught me that working together towards common goals could be realized by anyone on the same mission—assuming they were on the same mission. In my experience at Raland, the missions were not always aligned.

When I fell ill, I suggested a partner take the helm of our company as the front-facing leader. I thought the idea of an outward-facing partner-type leadership was detrimental to our growth because there was no one person responsible for the success or failure of the company. I also felt that my being afflicted with MS could be looked at as a liability by potential clients. I later concluded this idea itself was actually a detriment to the company.

The management style my partner chose to use pitted employee against employee in a failed attempt to cause the company divisions to work harder at outdoing each other; a kind of friendly competition. On the surface, it may have sounded good, but the results showed differently. It was a fool's game, resulting in disharmony and internal strife paired with reduced company profits.

In the military, we learned the concept of a team of specialists working together towards the same mission, helping one another achieve overarching goals for the betterment of all. However, pitting people against people is not only counter-productive but just bad business no matter the size of the organization.

When I received complaints from my employees, I took a deeper look into what I had been missing. I knew we were having some internal problems, but what I found disturbed me. I flew to Washington, DC from our office in New York to meet and discuss the company's issues with my partner. But more so, to consider what we needed to do to fix the situation. I felt we could fix things. His leadership style was an attempt at creating a division of people that would make the company stronger. It just didn't work.

Our conversation was amenable and respectful. He apologized for the issues created. His capitulation amazed me. After all, his management style was to create strife in an attempt at control and growth. He was waving a white flag of surrender with no discourse, which was unfortunate, but I accepted his decision. Even with his submission, it was never my goal to topple him. My goal was only to correct the situation and move forward. I liked him and wanted success for all.

I said to him, "We can fix the situation, and no one needs to know about our meeting. We will work together to correct the style, patch the holes, and right the wrongs. We will be okay as a company." I expected that he would think about our conversation and realize that we could fix the issues.

He didn't. He submitted his intent to separate from the partnership ten days later.

I took the helm but still felt the outward-facing company image should not be of a person with an illness. I was wrong, and time would prove this.

Lessons Learned

- **First and foremost: never give in, give up or be counted out.**

- **Illnesses of any type make people uncomfortable.** When people are uncomfortable, they can act out in different ways, sometimes from ignorance and sometimes from hostility. I have found that most act out because of ignorance.

- **Be the pilot**, not the baggage handler.

EIGHT
Everything Changes

MULTIPLE SCLEROSIS MAKES ONE MORE SENSITIVE to extreme changes in temperature. I had been very blessed to be able to travel around the country chasing a year of perpetual spring. I would live in my Arizona home during the cold months and travel to the northeast during the heat of the summer. It worked and allowed for a more comfortable life, enabling me to meet the rigors of running a business that operated around the globe.

Multiple Sclerosis is not a prevalent condition in the western Arizona desert because of the effect heat has on individuals with the disease. Heat can be a catalyst for a relapse of symptoms or debilitating fatigue. For me personally, a great amount of heat, the heat of a desert in the summer can be very debilitating, robbing me of strength and endurance. This may well be the reason there are so few sufferers of the disease willing to live in such a climate. However, extreme cold can have similar effects, so I try to mitigate my problem the only way I can: I look for uninterrupted springtime temperatures.

I fell really ill in January 2011. At this time, I was wintering at my home in Arizona. Early in the month, I was losing my balance and often falling against the walls in our home's hallways. I was bouncing side to side when no one could see me. This fight to stand would make me angry, and because of stubbornness, and not accepting the fact I had a major chronic condition, I did not ask for help or let anyone know about my problem. This was a huge mistake.

After fighting this balance and strength problem for a few weeks, I decided to visit a friend who also happened to be the only neurologist in town.

My MS caused the issues. My neurologist friend did some testing and initially prescribed heavy doses of prednisone in an attempt to stabilize my condition before conducting an MRI. A few days later, I was able to get the recommended MRI, however by this time I could hardly stand. He shifted my treatment to infused steroids, but the results of the MRI showed things had gotten very serious.

He said it was beyond local expertise to deal with my condition and immediately transferred me to one of the largest names in MS Neurology who was located at the Mayo Clinic in Scottsdale, Arizona. This was a terrible time and altered my life in many ways.

A medical transport company with specialty EMTs picked me up from the local hospital and flew me to the clinic in Scottsdale. By the time I landed at the Mayo Clinic, I was fully paralyzed. I could not move my right arm, hand, leg, foot—everything on the right side of my body was completely dead.

The hospital sent me to the stroke unit because there was no other area even close to being capable of providing the care I needed. There, they pumped me with high-dose steroids day after day. One gram per day, which is roughly 100 times the dose of prednisone given for general inflammation. It is a very rough regime that affects everything in your body.

It really messes with your mind and body in ways that are hard to describe. I experienced "Incredible-Hulk" type rage, then sunk into whimpering depression. High doses of the drugs caused many side effects, including insomnia, and for me caused an incredible increase in the growth rate of my hair... I went from a clean-cut professional to "*Sasquatch*" in a matter of days. After infusing 10 grams of steroids with no improvement of symptoms, the doctors initially decided I should learn to live with my newfound paralysis. I was moved from the neurologic stroke unit to an in-house physical rehabilitation center to focus on physical and occupational therapy.

While lying in the hospital, unable to move, I had plenty of time to think. Much thought occurred in the late hours of the night when the hospital was at its quietest period.

I was dissatisfied with a couple of aspects of my life and business. In business, I was dissatisfied with my allowing partners too much control, not achieving all I wanted for my company. But I also had great happiness and satisfaction.

I felt so incredibly blessed despite my current situation. I had been raised by wonderful parents during an incredible time in history. I had experienced more in my five decades than most do in a lifetime. I traveled the world and completed everything I had set out to do. I had personal relationships with some of the best and brightest in the world. I had made discoveries, created solutions, and in the process, made history a time or two. I had married an astonishing woman, who was my biggest cheerleader in life. I had a great son and stepdaughter. I had nothing to feel sorry about—other than the prospect of not being able to reach what I determined was my full potential.

After a lot of consultation with every available expert on my condition, the physicians decided to try something that might help me; a procedure known as Plasmapheresis. This procedure takes the liquid part of your blood, also known as plasma, and mechanically separates it from the blood cells. It's like having dialysis, even using the same equipment. But it was physically very difficult for me. This process replaced my plasma with donor plasma.

The procedure was difficult, and on several occasions, it put me into shock. However, after a month of treatments, the regimen was complete, and to everyone's amazement, I could feel a little more on my right side. I was convinced that I would walk again even though I still could not get myself out of bed without help. I just needed to work at it and push myself during physical therapy.

I decided if I could get out of bed and move again, I would do something bigger and better than anything I had done in the past. I was truly going to change the world and help people. I had invented a product with which I had started the patent process. RxFusion would help people, but at this solution was not at the level I was envisioning. I needed to do something bigger, better, more impactful. I decided that if I could get out of the hospital and recover enough, I would roll my wheelchair and eventually walk to make this happen. My doctors were not as optimistic. They told me that the chance of walking was limited, if even possible, and that I should think about retiring.

I didn't follow my doctors' recommendation.

My Mission in the Wheelchair

Much changed after leaving the Mayo Clinic in the spring of 2011. I spent days undergoing physical therapy and nights dreaming of getting back into the game. My body was a mess, but I focused my mind on getting a major win. I wanted to do what I had promised myself during those long nights in the Mayo. I wanted to do something bigger, better, and more impactful. I needed to find my purpose.

My amazing caregivers had been outraged when I conducted meetings from my hospital bed, effectively running my company while *"I was supposed to be healing."* I did this by phone and email and on several occasions, had key individuals fly in for face-to-face meetings. The doctors and nurses constantly reminded me that the hospital is a place to heal. I understood this, but healing is a combination activity—mind and body!

I hadn't improved much by the time of my discharge. Yes, I had started to feel more on my right side, but I still could not move without aid. I left the clinic still unable to walk without a person standing next to me, holding me up with either a mechanism or with straps. I was paralyzed head to toe on the right side of my body. I could barely move my right arm, just a few inches at best, while undergoing therapy during my last couple weeks at the clinic; that was all.

I left the Mayo Clinic unable to walk, but I would receive out-patient rehabilitation closer to home to continue working on my healing. A welcome, yet scary prospect. Knowing that Pat would not have the assistance provided by a full-time hospital staff, I was faced with the reality I would be alone at times, and unable to care for myself should anything go wrong. And things, little things, did go wrong. It was a big adjustment as Pat and I started to work into a routine, interrupted by my trips for physical therapy.

About a month after discharge, I returned for a well-visit checkup at the Mayo Clinic. It was on this visit that I did a little showing off for the caregivers who had so steadfastly dealt with how difficult I had been as a patient. When I arrived at the floor, which I had for too long a time called home, my caregivers circled around my wheelchair to see how I was doing. I smiled and told them I had been working hard, and I would continue to advance. I shared stories of progress and setbacks but wanted to show them something.

I stood up from my wheelchair without assistance, to cheers and tears.

A Diagnosis is Not the End of Life

One might think this would be the end of my story. It wasn't.

When I look back on this moment, I see it was really just the start. The start of a new and bigger story. One which would take me from the depths of despair and doubt to the heights of victory many times over. Success and failure can be as simple as a decision.

For a person who has paralysis, victory can come in the form of standing and walking unaided. Or standing on the biggest stage in entrepreneurship as a recovering patient. It can come in the knowledge you are helping to inspire someone or in achieving scientific breakthroughs that so many said were impossible.

Victory can come from being asked to write for an international publication or responding to an email from an ailing patient seeking comfort.

For me, victory is doing and doing something impactful. Something that can truly change a person's life for the better.

Moving forward, I decided to live again. Within three months of discharge, as the desert was heating up to a full-summer boil, we headed back to the Northeast for relief and to get back into the game. I wanted to get back to work full time and make a difference.

Small Steps

The first day in New York may have been a rainy, dreary occasion; however, for me, it was a grand and glorious day. I achieved a personal victory that day when we pulled up to my office. I got out of the vehicle and into my wheelchair, and had a walker handy to allow me to walk into my office standing up; a goal I had set for myself while still in the physical therapy unit at the Mayo Clinic. This one small daily task able-bodied people take for granted and never think about was a victory for me.

I walked in, aided, yes, but upright. It was difficult, but I knew to heal and increase the strength I needed to do this as much as possible. However, not all people understand the idea of these personal victories.

A person in the office made it clear they did not want to see me using a walker in the office. I don't know if they thought I was weak in spirit and could be controlled, but they took me aside and told me I should use my wheelchair because the walker made some people in the office uncomfortable. Needless to say, I was more than perplexed by this suggestion. It showed a person who was weak or had issues with those who were disabled. I knew with absolute confidence, things were going to change internally, and this person was only there for a paycheck.

It was also a time I was able to start living again. I shook off the statements and did as I pleased. I would use my walker, cane, or wheelchair as needed, or as I saw fit. Hell, I owned the company. No one would dictate my actions in *my* office. My goal was to continue to grow the company and build things. But also, to meet the commitments I made to myself during those late nights in the Mayo Clinic.

I shifted focus to find exactly what I was looking for. It had to be big, bold, and game-changing. It had to help the masses in ways never thought possible before. I did not know what "it" was, but I was determined to find it.

I traveled the eastern seaboard looking for possibilities. I spent time at places like Johns Hopkins University, reviewing available intellectual property. But nothing stood out as the "it" idea. I wanted a big, bold, game-changing challenge: one that was not only revolutionary but would improve the lives of people.

Not finding what I was looking for on my own, I started networking again. I went to a meeting of local executives in Rochester, New York, known as "Pariemus." At this meeting, I met Julie, who would steer me into the biggest effort of my life. Julie is a connector, a person who listens to your ideas, and connects you to a person who might be able to assist in your goals. And she made a connection for me. Her information led me to meet with a person from the University of Rochester who had suffered a great personal tragedy himself decades earlier. In fact, his tragedy and triumph made both the *Reader's Digest* magazine in the mid-1970s and the television program "I Survived" decades later. He knew and understood my challenges and motivations. He was just the person I needed to meet.

I received a call a week later from a University of Rochester physician/researcher, Spencer Rosero. He had an idea he wanted to discuss with me. We set an appointment and met in my conference room on a cloudy afternoon in the fall of 2011.

Spencer is a well-spoken, highly intelligent person who has a way of immediately connecting with people. His mannerisms are that of an approachable genius. He pulled out prototypes and data related to his discovery. He talked about his invention and described areas where he felt it needed improvement. He had such a genuine and positive style I quickly knew I had found a partner for my next venture.

Spencer and I decided to merge our ideas and form a company where we would move our discoveries forward to market. I did a lot of thinking. Spencer is a busy person working as a top physician and researcher. I had experience from years of starting and growing business, but this would be different. So different, I wanted to backfill my experience and knowledge with that of others. I decided to do things differently again.

I left my old playbook behind and did something bold. I started to build a boardroom. My "Billion Dollar Boardroom."

Building a Board of Directors

Let's start with an observation: Not every company needs a board of directors. However, some companies benefit from having a group of people outside of the organization who can oversee and provide guidance to the in-house leadership. Boards can be either extremely useful or potentially detrimental to a company.

In a recent conversation, I spoke to a person who was consulting to the board of directors for a company who had some internal issues. He told me that to his amazement, the company's board had no expertise in a business like the one they were charged with guiding. In this case, the board was detrimental to the health and well-being of the company. The board members understood nothing about what the company did and therefore had no expertise to assist.

This issue spoke to the way the leadership, who had recruited the board, ran the company and the predicaments it faced. It also highlighted the thought process one must go through before recruiting and seating a board of directors. It is important the people you select provide value: they should be experts in their respective fields and have experience in the industry in which your company is operating.

I wanted to bring people into our efforts who were already successful and knowledgeable. I knew I lacked experience running a huge company, which I envisioned Efferent Labs would become. I wanted to make sure to bring in people who had this proficiency. Raland was good sized (for a small company), but I knew that Efferent Labs would be much larger at some point. I wanted experienced, big company people seated next to me to help guide me down the path of growth.

My billion-dollar boardroom needed Fortune 500 players. CEOs, CFOs, and CMOs. I needed the best and brightest. I reached out through my network and platforms like LinkedIn. I sent emails, made phone calls, and connected through social media.

I had several conversations with board candidates and settled on a few select, high-profile individuals. One was the former CEO and President of major corporations like Palm, Reebok, Cadbury-Schweppes and the former COO and President of Sony Electronics.

He had the experience I could call on as we grew. He knew the inner working of large corporations, and I needed his experience on my team. I reached out to him through LinkedIn. He referred me to a friend for vetting, another CEO. I had a conversation with his friend who must have determined that I was okay, as my candidate sent an invitation for a phone meeting a few days later.

During a local meet-up with the Pariemus group again, I met another individual, an accomplished Chief Marketing Officer (CMO). We talked and quickly found common goals. I invited him to join our efforts as well.

My new CMO friend knew several people, one being the Chief Financial Officer (CFO) for major corporations. He provided me with the CFO's contact information, and I sent an introductory email. The email led to a phone call. I rounded the board off with the CEO and physician of a major hospital. My efforts had yielded an impressive group of accomplished professionals.

My boardroom would meet for the first time, and it made the front-page, above the fold news in the local business journal. This was not by accident.

I wanted to alert local investors that a new entrepreneur was in town—one who would stir things up with something worth looking into for investment. I reached out to the business journal and, more specifically, one of their experienced reporters, offering him an exclusive.

I told him I was having the inaugural meeting of my board, and it had some big names. If he wanted the exclusive, he needed to do a few things. One, guarantee front-page placement, preferably above the fold, and two, be available for interviews after the board meeting, which was to take place on a Saturday. This was a large lift for the reporter: he would be giving up some of his free time for a story which would take time and a lot of effort to write, but he was there on schedule.

His story was well researched and covered the angles I was hoping to put out. It appeared in print the next week.

The Pitch

The next fall, Spencer and I went out to pitch our new company to local investors with no success. My efforts with the business journal got us in the door, but pitching the company and getting an investment took more than a good record of success and a billion-dollar boardroom. In fact, the boardroom was a deterrent for some investors. They questioned why we would need their money with such a powerful board. This was a question I had never considered while preparing for the pitch.

When building my board, I specifically wanted one to guide and direct, but not necessarily invest their money. I felt their experience was more valuable and important to the success of the company. And I also mistakenly thought if I had such a heavy-weight board, people would be falling all over each other to invest, and I would be turning people away at the door. This turned out to be more fantasy than fact.

It also meant I would need to hit the road and find the investors myself.

Spencer and I would go on to pitch dozens of times to similar audiences with similar responses: too early, not enough done, you will never pull this off, it's science fiction. I have heard these comments dozens of times over more than 100 pitches since we founded our start-up.

I wrote a story for *Forbes* about pitching in August of 2016:

Forbes—August 2016
Shark Tank Is Not Even Close To Reality: How This Entrepreneur Prepares For A Pitch

The Reality of a Pitch

In this brave new world of TV pitch shows like ABC's Shark Tank and CNBC's The West Texas Investors Club, entrepreneurs from all walks of life are led to believe that the pitch is like a television reality show.

News flash! It's not. Maybe it should be—it would be more fun for both pitcher and pitchee—but again, it is not even close, at least not in my experience of pitching to hundreds of individuals over the last few years.

In my life as a start-up CEO I do a lot of presenting. I pitch for everything: investment, partnership, prize money, you name it. Each presentation is as unique as are the individuals being pitched. However, the basic elements that go into the pitch are pretty standard: PowerPoint deck, big font, few words, quick to the point.

During a pitch, investors are trying to understand your offering, gather some information about what the deal might look like, and then make a decision as to whether or not to take a deeper dive into what your offering. If they get a good feeling about you and your product, and like the deal you are presenting, they may ask for a more in-depth look at your company. Usually, a short 10-15-minute pitch is the rule on the angel side, a longer and more detailed presentation for the venture capital community.

The investors are expecting you to provide value for their time. You must respect the time and effort the investor is providing by being factual and direct. They look at hundreds of deals a year, so you want them to have a positive recollection of your presentation.

I always put myself in their position—how would I react, watching some guy asking me to open my checkbook? Respect their time, and even if you get a no on your first try, you can and may be invited back for another go, if your company is still around at a later date.

Over the last half decade or so I have watched a wholesale shift in early investment: Friends and family are the new angel investors. The angel investor acts more like the venture capitalist (VC) of the past—tolerant of little risk and wanting a quick return at a high multiplier. I have also noted that the VC today now tends to operate much more like an institutional investor.

Preparing For a Yes

In the weeks prior to a pitch, I gather a small team to review past presentations. We talk about the good and bad of the last few presentations and then rip everything apart and start over. Doing a postmortem of the last pitch is a must. You know the old adage "those who forget the past..."

We then look at our next audience, get to understand the group or person, and reformulate our pitch to our understanding of their expectations. So our process always looks like this:

- Postmortem
- Research
- Construct the pitch
- Practice
- Reformulate the pitch—because it is not as good as it sounded when you put it on paper the first time, then

- Practice
- Practice
- -Practice

When I walk in the door to pitch, I want to be able to talk clearly about my business, offering it in terms and details that will win an investment, or at least a second look. You could be manufacturing pure gold for pennies on the dollar, and the investors will give you a hundred reasons why your gold is worthless, and no one would ever want it. You want them to understand what you inherently understand: your business or product is going to be the best.

After years of preparing, practicing and pitching I found a very good source of the "how" of the pitch.

If you are planning to present to investors, I recommend that you buy and read Guy Kawasaki's "The Art of the Start 2.0" and the use it as a guide. It is a comprehensive tool to construct and deliver a good pitch. Guy lays out the how's and whys in his book, but it is in your own research you will learn what will be key in your pitch. Just as important—you still have to pitch in your own voice.

Just as Guy recommends, I try to keep my pitch simple. I also work to pitch in terms of three. No more than three ideas on a slide, and get to the end with three major takeaways, that's it.

In my life experience, most people can digest and remember only three things reasonably well, in a single serving—so keep it simple.

Hope Is Not a Plan

In my preparations, I don't hope for a yes; I plan for it. If you don't believe that you can get a yes, you will project that in a subconscious way. If you believe in yourself first, your product second, and your company third, you can and will get a yes— maybe not today, but you will get it.

After months of pitching, we were able to refine our presentation. Communication is very important no matter what you are doing. In a pitch, your ability to communicate a vision is especially important, or within a few seconds you will lose your audience and it's over. Over before it really even starts.

I think the last straw for us was when we auditioned to pitch to an investor group. I thought we nailed it. The pitch, I felt, was spot on. The ideas were clearly delivered and the traction of the company, although minimal at that time, was starting to take shape. The chairman of the committee, who determined those who would pitch to the larger committee, pulled me aside to talk after the Q&A session had concluded. He said that we did well enough to pitch but cautioned me we just needed more of a story to actually get an investment. At that time, I felt beat down.

Like all other young companies, we felt we had everything. All the boxes were checked, and heck, I even had what other start-ups didn't have, a billion-dollar boardroom. But none of that mattered. We needed more. I didn't accept the committee's offer to pitch. We decided to work on our product more, and also to refine our pitch again.

To refine our story, we needed to answer the questions asked by those who watched pitches all the time. They knew what is expected by investors. We needed to communicate in a way that investors expect and understand. Spencer and I would spend a lot of time learning how to communicate an idea while refining our pitch.

43North

I have worked through life creating my personal Venn, one piece at a time. But it was with the legal formation of Efferent Labs in October 2013, that I felt the results of decades of struggle and lessons learned were culminating in a calling which would bear even more and sweeter fruit.

Pitching so many investors at so many events led me to New York City in the spring of 2014. At the time we were on the road, traveling from our winter home in Arizona to Rochester to escape the heat of the upcoming summer. Pat and I were in our standard transit route, taking a short break in Charleston, South Carolina, when I received an email from the Director of New York MedTech, informing me they had an opening to pitch at an event in a little over a week. The event was being held in New York City, so to reduce flight times, we relocated to North Carolina, where I would fly to New York while Pat did business development for Raland in the Research Triangle Park area.

I became familiar with MedTech as a Central New York State based trade organization. I had started a little group in Rochester a couple summers prior to promote life science networking in the region which I named "ROC City BioBeers." The MedTech Director had reached out to introduce me to her organization and offered to sponsor one of our events.

I happily accepted her offer because either myself or a co-founder had carried much of the costs for the networking events to date, and I was more than happy to have a sponsor this time around. At that event, she also tried to recruit me to her organization, but I was hesitant. The reason I had started

ROC City BioBeers was that there was no one doing these type events for our industry in the Western New York area. I appreciated the sponsorship, and I ended up joining the MedTech organization.

I reached out to my board chairman, Carl Yankowski, to see if he wanted to attend the pitch with me in New York City. I felt Carl would be a good backup should people have questions about the company's long-term prospects, and he lived in near proximity to the city. They gave me ten minutes pitch time, with a standard question-and-answer period to follow.

Overall, I felt that my pitch went well. I was amongst peers and most of them seemed to get our company's concept. Questions were good, and the conversations after told me I had done extremely well in my presentation. It was then I made the contact who started a chain of events which still resonates to this day.

I met a nice lady from the University at Buffalo, Kim. She asked me a very interesting question:

"Do you know about the 43North contest?"

I told her I had heard of the contest and thought about entering but hesitated to do so. She asked why? I told her I was older in age and didn't have a hip new app that the contest was probably focusing on. I knew the media had reported that there were hundreds of entries already, and I felt my chances were not worth the time it would take to enter.

She informed me that the contest was looking for "exactly what you are doing!" and encouraged me to enter.

When I arrived at the Raland offices in Rochester in late May 2014, I thought about my encounter with Kim. I looked at the calendar and noted that I had a little over a week to get my application submitted. I registered on-line and opened the contest application, but let it sit for days as other items of greater importance were piled on my desk.

Just Do It

On the last day to enter, I decided to get serious and submit my application. I reviewed each line in the application answering the questions. It was fairly easy because I had most of the answers handy from my pitch decks. A simple cut and paste was really all I needed to do. I answered questions all afternoon and into the evening. If I would do this, I was going to do it right and at least get something submitted that would be a contender.

I quickly assessed my odds that night, not knowing that thousands of companies from across the globe were doing the same thing. I had believed the number was closer to a few hundred as reported earlier in the month. I thought I would definitely be better than two-thirds of the applicants just out of the gates. It was a few weeks later that I found out that over 9,600 entries had been entered for consideration.

I believed that at least I did my best and now it was up to the contest judges to pick out the semi-finalists for the next stage of the competition. I sent an email to my UB contact, Kim, and told her I did enter after all.

The Big Move

In August 2014, I received an email from 43North informing they had selected us as a semi-finalist. We had made the first cut. I quickly emailed Kim to tell her the exciting news. She had read the notification online and knew we had been selected the same time I did. Our emails crossed in the cloud, and I received her congratulations note at the same time she received my email. The first time I ever experienced that occurrence!

The next round would be one where Spencer and I would do a video pitch to the contest judges. This occurred about three weeks later. It was this pitch that would make or break us with this competition.

I prepared a pitch that met the requirements of the contest, and when the day came to pitch, Spencer and I sat in front of my computer screen and did our best. The video pitch ended with a "thank you, you will be informed if we decide to advance you." That was it. There was no feedback on our presentation, but we both felt we had done a good job and were planning for our next pitch. In a video pitch, you can't gauge your performance by looking at the audience.

This was also about the time I was planning my return trip to Arizona for the winter. I would work from Arizona, traveling as necessary to support the efforts of Efferent and of Raland. This year was no different, with one exception. They might select us as a finalist.

A finalist was guaranteed a cash prize investment of at least $250,000, but like all the other applicants, we were only interested in the $1,000,000 grand prize. With that much money in hand, we could advance our technology much faster.

The Call

It was in our return trek across the United States to Arizona that I had my first indication we might have been selected to advance in the contest. At the most inopportune time, an email came in. The organizers of the 43North contest said that we were being considered as a finalist and we needed to complete some additional paperwork to allow them to make a determination. We were driving down the interstate in the middle of nowhere. We pulled over and quickly completed all the qualifying information and then needed to locate a fax machine to return it to the competition.

Two weeks later I received a phone call. The call was short but sweet.

***

I wrote more about the 43North experience in my *Forbes* column:

Forbes—August 2016
How I Won $500,000 For My Start-up

Everyone knows that ideas are a dime a dozen. The difference between an idea and a business is money and execution. Lots of money. A whole lot of good execution, but lots of money too.

Running Low On Cash

In May 2014, I was pretty much out of money for my start-up Efferent Labs. My co-founder and I had invested a lot of our own money and resources, and had made great progress with our product, an implantable sensor to monitor cellular function from within the patient. However, we hit a wall raising money—too early for many investors, and not in the investment space for all the others we pitched.

Opportunity Knocks

I received an invitation from the MedTech organization (the NY State Life Science Industry Organization) and was offered a slot to pitch my company in New York City to local investors during the "MedTech Metro" event. I jumped at the offer. It is imperative to recognize an opportunity when it is presented, and act on it. Execute or die.

I arrived in New York City knowing only when and where I should show up. When I got to the venue, I found that there were two other companies pitching that evening and I was slated to go last—a position I like, because directly after my pitch, I am able to talk to investors who still have my story fresh at the top of their minds.

The audience had a lot of good questions and I could make some interesting acquaintances. But the connection I made that ended up being the goldmine for me was not an investor, but rather a University at Buffalo business development executive. She had listened carefully to my presentation and wanted to chat.

The Connector

The business development executive from University at Buffalo approached me and asked if I had heard of the 43North competition out of Buffalo, NY. I had, but thought I might not be the best fit—we are not inventing an app, and I self-identified as "old guy." I thought the competition was designed for millennials creating apps. We chatted and exchanged business cards, and I promised to re-look at the competition. She encouraged me to submit an application, stating that we were "exactly what they are looking for." In the final hours of the final day to enter, I did.

She was right! From the 9,600 applications originating from 96 countries and all 50 states, they selected us as one of the 113 semi-finalists! Even better, after a video pitch and an additional in-depth application, we were notified that we were a finalist with a guaranteed prize, competing for the grand prize of one million dollars. This was great news! We had the opportunity to showcase our company and great discoveries in front of an international audience, and at a minimum, we would walk away with a quarter million dollars in investment. If we beat everyone else, we could grab the grand prize which could fund us for almost two years, getting our medical device close to market.

The Competition

I arrived in Buffalo the last week of October 2014, ready to compete. After a couple days touring the Buffalo area and ecosystem, mentoring sessions and introductions, the day of the contest was upon us. The contest was to take place on the stage of the Shea Performing Arts Center in downtown Buffalo. The Shea is a grand venue that opened in 1926 and has a seating capacity over 4,000. The stage was huge, so large as to house the entire pitch competition on a "stage on the stage", with around 300 gallery observers. It was an intimidating setup, with seven judges from industry, investment and media closely reviewing and questioning each presentation. Strict rules on timing were enforced by an MC (an investor himself), who could hook you off the stage if you ran over time. The entire contest was broadcast on large screens in the theater and simulcast online throughout the world.

Our time to pitch came in the afternoon. We were third from the last to present, so there was a lot of time to let our nerves take charge. We were outfitted backstage with wireless microphones and given last-minute instructions by the production crew.

I felt good, but a member of the crew asked me if I wanted an *Altoid* mint. I didn't understand why at the time and declined; however, I quickly learned why it was offered when I stepped on stage. All I can say is, if you are offered an *Altoid* before presenting to a large crowd, accept it graciously. Within seconds of standing on the stage before the world, my mouth went as dry as the desert, something I had never before experienced.

In spite of the dry mouth, my presentation went great, and the question-and-answer period was equally great. We exited the stage and could feel a win in our bones.

The Time Of Reckoning

After a few hours of evaluation, the judges had reached their decisions; the stage was transformed, and a much larger audience had assembled in the main theatre. We contestants were lined up alphabetically behind stage awaiting our fate. Because of my disability, they stationed me just behind the curtains near the front of the stage. The judges were positioned next to me, and I was able to briefly chat with the main life science judge, who expressed his support for what we were doing.

To increase the drama of the finals, and not wanting any competitor to know their exact position in the competition, the winnings were handed out in reverse alphabetical order, based on award amount. The first prizes awarded were the four quarter-million-dollar amounts. As each winner was announced, they claimed their prize and took two steps back, then the front line shifted to stage left, getting shorter with each announcement. There was a huge sigh of relief by those of us still standing after the fourth and final quarter-million-dollar winner was announced; everyone left standing on the front line still had a shot at the million-dollar prize.

After they announced a few more names, our dream of the million-dollar grand prize did not materialize. We had won a $500,000 investment for five percent of our company, a huge amount and at the time one of the largest contest awards in the world for start-up companies. We were thrilled!

Winning Is A Great Thing

Just when we had hit the low of too many "Nos", we hit the grand "Yes." We won a half million dollars and a lot of other perks, including free office space and tax-free status as part of the Start-up NY program. In the 18 months since arriving in Buffalo, we are making incredible progress and are getting closer each day to entering our market.

What seemed a near impossibility has proven to be the best move we made with our company to date. Since our win, we have made great strides towards our goal of helping people who are suffering from the effects of cancer chemotherapy.

I later learned that we were not only a $500,000 winner, but we were number two in the overall selection. We had come extremely close to winning the million-dollar prize. Although they attempted to mask the actual order of the winners, I later learned that out of the 9,600 entries, we ended up second in the overall competition.

So even though we didn't win the grand prize, I did what anyone wanting to win a million dollars and getting halfway there would do. I worked to double the effect of the money. I submitted for and gained a couple of matching grants to supercharge our winnings.

* * *

Lessons Learned

- **Not every company needs a board of directors.** In my case, I knew I would need one and built one very early in the formation of Efferent Labs. Some might contend I formed a board too early. In hindsight, I may have been a little aggressive in establishing the formal board so early, but the benefit has been that all board members have been part of the growth of the company since day one. They have all experienced my ups and downs and have been there to assist me as needed in moving the company forward.

- **Use the news media as a marketing arm.** The media can assist in getting your word out at no cost. In a start-up, the costs associated with advertising can be difficult to deal with. If you use the media when something noteworthy occurs, you will have a marketing arm that provides a great way to forward your message. The news outlet will decide if your story is worth the time and cost to tell, and it is good to let them be the decision-maker in that aspect.

- **When pitching, you will not know every answer,** but you can listen to every question and if needed, capture the question for follow-up at a later time. When preparing for your pitch, try to envision different challenging questions based on your particular experience. Always offer a follow-up to a question you are unsure of the answer to—never wing it—the investor will recognize it immediately and no longer be interested in investing. In the investor's eye, you have proven to be less than trustworthy.

NINE
Networking

IKE ANYONE, I CAN FIND MYSELF SITTING in my office, staring at the computer screen. Zoning out in my personal comfort zone.

Everyone does this.

It's an average day, in an average week.

You are sitting at your desk.

It is another day, of another week, of another year.

This is probably the most common thing that happens to people at work. Books have been written about this phenomenon. Why? Because it happens to everyone.

The screen is glaring in your face with a bunch of letters, numbers, PowerPoints, or emails burning into both the display and your retinas.

Your mind starts to wander, and you feel entirely useless.

The minutes stretch to an hour, and you start to panic because you know that time is something you will never get back. Time is precious, and the wasting of it in today's fast-paced, on-demand environment can cause the panicky feeling of being mired in minutia. You just want to throw your hands in the air and leave. You should.

Get Out of Your Comfort Zone

It was one of these days in the fall of 2017 where I found myself lost in a pile of things to accomplish, and feeling overwhelmed with so much on my plate, I didn't know what to do next.

I threw my hands in the air. But I didn't retreat. No, that would not have solved my problem. I got up from my desk, and within a half-hour had done more this day than most people do in a week. In the many hours leading up to the point of pushing my chair back and realizing I had been wasting my time, I lost valuable opportunities. Not anymore.

I wrote a story about this issue and the results of my actions in my column for *Inc.* that evening:

Inc.—September 2017
This Daily Habit Will Help Your Business Thrive

Although it is not very popular with most start-up founders because of the demands of starting a company, getting out of the office is probably the best thing you, as an entrepreneur, can do to aid in your business growth and ultimate success.

I use the word network a lot, and for good reason. Networking develops relationships and relationships are the keys to building, growing, and sustaining the progression of your company.

When I was constructing my last company, I didn't want to spend any money by attending trade shows, or for that matter, travel anywhere without some sort of guarantee I would see a financial return "right now" for the effort and expense.

This attitude cost me dearly during the first couple of years of my previous company. My actions kept the company from being exposed to potential customers and those customers from learning about our great offerings. Obviously, if you're not a real social person, or maybe even a bit introverted, you might say that networking is outside your comfort zone. Well, you signed up to be an entrepreneur, so it's time to get social! I know you may be asking: But how?

Get out of your office

Start by just leaving your office. In my case, I merely need to walk outside and down the street a block to "get social". Just yesterday I felt the need to get out for a while, and when I did, I ran into seven people over my period of 35 minutes out and about. Seven people I might not have had the opportunity of talking to if I had stayed in my office.

I spoke to all, got actionable information from two, made a lunch date with a third, a plan to connect next week with a fourth and planned an email exchange follow-up from a fifth. Five out of the seven contacts I made resulted in something well worth the 35 minutes I spent away from my desk. This would not have happened if I didn't leave my office.

Why is this live human interaction important?

A chance, unplanned and a quick catch-up is often better than an email or phone call. The reason is simple—you place a face with an idea. This causes a sensory response. The live meet creates a memory with a much deeper connection. Unlike an email, the memory cannot be deleted with the click of a mouse.

I often propose writing and mailing letters, not emails, for the same reason. In the case of a mailed letter, the recipient must perform an action much deeper in thought and deed than a simple click with a mouse. First, they look at the envelope— something that is rarely done today since everyone is too busy to write a letter—then they must open the letter, read it and decide an action. A much longer, neural connected action.

There is a real effort required and interaction created by opening and reading a letter. It is much greater than the effort used in reading email, and therefore the probability of the recipient taking action increases proportionally.

The same is true with a face-to-face encounter over a text or phone call. You connect on several levels, even for a short period of time, and will have a much higher probability of action and follow-up.

If you aren't located in the center of an active a business community as I am—one that could result in the chance meetings on the street like I had yesterday—you can always look online for a "meet-up" or other live networking event that might place you in the vicinity of others in your area of interest.

Planting the seeds for growth

You can look at this as planting seeds for the future. When I started networking more, over a decade ago, I quickly saw the rewards. Chance meetings created business opportunities, which in turn created revenue. The revenues continued to grow over time as the seeds sprouted, formed roots and grew into better relationships.

Today I live by this rule on a daily basis. I put myself in the middle of at least one unique and potentially fruitful networking situation daily. I meet people at events, set follow-on meetings and then work the opportunity at hand.

Will all opportunities I create bear fruit? I hope so! However, if I had never planted the seeds, watered and tended to them, there would be nothing but barren land in front of me rather than the current blooming orchard of possibilities.

So, travel, network, get the heck out of your office. The rewards for your business will far outweigh the small amount of effort.

My Actions Made a Difference

My short trek gave me something I wasn't finding while I was looking at the computer screen: engagement. As an entrepreneur, you must engage others and find what you may not even know you are looking for. All the engagements you make will not bear fruit; however, they all don't need to, just some of them.

* * *

The engagement I described in the article for *Inc.* is just about networking. Networking is an art that can be learned. And like any art, it requires practice to become skilled.

I took my years of networking experience and wrote an article for *Forbes* in June 2017, which talks about the "how-to" of networking. This article was a very popular piece and was awarded the "Editors Pick" for content and popularity.

Forbes—June 2017
Effective Networking Requires Work.
How To Make The Most Of Every Event

Throughout my years, I have found that networking is an effective tool that can be used to build a business. Through my own trial and error, I have identified what methods work consistently for any networking event.

People are people

As a rule, people tend to be reserved, and more often than not, a bit shy. For most people, it is hard to enter a room full of strangers and engage them. It is those that can pull the veil of privacy down just a little who find the best results in a networking situation.

Rules to follow

To effectively network, you must do a little upfront homework. This is part of your job, so treat it as such. Done right, networking is work. Here are some of the basics to create an event that will provide value to you.

1. Look in your area for events where there might be a benefit for your company or to you as a person. In cities large and small, events happen on a weekly basis. In an average month I get invited to dozens of events, and read about dozens of others. With this huge barrage of possibilities, you need to focus on your business goals, and attend the events that support those goals.

2. Identify your networking goals. If you go to an event without at least a loose set of goals, you are not going to benefit much. Sure, you might grab a bite of the standard event fare and a beer, but you will have wasted what could have been a major opportunity. Some examples of goals might include: make contact with a potential partner or customer, or find out what makes the completion tick. Whatever your specific needs are, review and list the top objectives of the event.

3. Prepare for the event. Why go if your event isn't going to advance your business agenda or meet your identified goals? Plan. This means learning not only about the event but also those who regularly attend the event. Review the event website, LinkedIn, and industry sites. Look for reviews of any past events. If they are available, sign up for newsletters connected with the event.

4. Do some online "pre-networking." Reach out to a few people you know that may have attended the event. Get familiar with the LinkedIn profiles of those you have found who have attended in the past. Try to connect to a couple potential contacts with a LinkedIn message letting them know you will be attending the event and would like to meet. This will give them the opportunity to get familiar with you through your profile. It also helps them to start thinking about how you might find similar interests or make introductions.

5. Identify your top three targets. Target contacts are the people you absolutely want to meet while attending. Familiarize yourself with your targets through available profiles, news items, or other information. Get familiar with any photo of targets so you can quickly identify them in a crowded room.

On day of event:

1. Grab a hand full of business cards. A small number of cards is all that is needed. If you are moving person-to-person handing out cards at the event, you are wasting your time and money. Focus on finding the people that will make a real impact towards your goals, starting with your pre-selected targets.

2. Show up a few minutes late—yes, late! Why? Well, if you arrive early, you will end up getting cornered by a person or group that will take too much of your time. If you arrive a little late, not only are early arrivals already engaged, more people have arrived, so you will be more likely to be able to mingle and find the people you had set as targets for meeting.

3. When you arrive, scan the room. Look for your target contacts first. Plan your movements and path so as to not get caught by unnecessary distractions. Take note of non-verbal cues when moving around the room. Remember, you are there with specific goals. Focus your networking on those goals.

4. Make the connection. Your target contacts are likely to be involved in conversations. Work your way over and do the "three-point stand." This move is basically positioning yourself to form a triangle and attempt to engage both people (as long as it is not a personal conversation). Make eye contact with your target. If your presence would place more than three people in the stand, move on. Too many people to be effective and you might get lost in the crowd. It is likely your three-point stand will cause the person you are not interested in speaking with to complete their conversation and move on. If that doesn't work or feels awkward, quickly abort and wait for the two to finish their conversation, then re-engage with the target.

5. Make your initial contact brief and work for a follow-up meet. It is important to not try to close a sale in a networking event unless the target leads you there. What you want to do is to engage, make a positive impression, provide a "teaser," and get the date. If you are networking correctly, they will ask you a couple questions, and this is where you simply exchange business cards.

Tell your target you would love to get a cup of coffee or meet at the office and chat a little more. Make the second date right then if you can. Then move on. Don't linger. Move away from the target. Look for your next target and do it all over again.

Always be prepared to give. Maybe the only thing you can do for your target is to offer a connection. Do it. The

W. K. (BILL) RADER

mileage gained from providing a good connection will be better than you might expect, and for me has always paid back with dividends.

6. Beware the "friend". Stay away from those who are looking to chat you up. Now, if they are one of your targets, they might have targeted you—Bingo! However, that is the exception to the rule and not very likely.

   If you run into personal or business friends, say hello, but quickly move on. You can chat anytime. Always be working your targets. At every event the "lonely attendee" will stop you. These are the people who look at a networking event to socialize rather than do real business. Be polite but keep moving. Take no more than 30 seconds, and if possible, introduce them to someone standing nearby, then politely move on.

7. Targets acquired and met; look for new contacts. When you have met your target contacts, you can spend a little time making new acquaintances and seeing if there are any potential collaborations. If the house is dry on potential collaborations, excuse yourself and head out. It's okay to leave early.

   It's best not to be the person who is overly available. Scarcity makes people more interested in meeting and working with you. If you gathered a bunch of business cards, take time to capture the key interests on the card right away. It might be a personal item or a business need. If you jot the information down now, you will look like a hero later.

After the event:

The closing step is the follow-up. This is where over 99% of network attendees fail. They go, they chat, they leave, and they don't use that valuable business card.

Long-term value, zero.

You must close your work. With the information you received at the event, you should go back and research. Your next meeting must have solutions or offers available that will make the people you targeted want to learn more and buy your offer. Call the targets and get a meeting.

* * *

I Value Networking

As illustrated in my stories for both *Forbes* and *Inc.*, I place great value in networking. Had I not used my skills in networking, I would never have been introduced to Spencer, my business partner and friend. I would not have met the people who would help me build my billion-dollar boardroom. I would also have missed out on meeting the person who would write stories about our enterprise, resulting in a lot of positive press.

The word "*work*" exists as an integral part of the word networking. It takes work to network correctly and obtain results with value. Approach networking events as your job, not a party. Use the same effort you use in running your company. If you work the event, you will leave with something of value.

It was in this *Forbes* story where I wrote more about networking results and gave lessons along the way:

Forbes—August 2016
Something Ventured Something Gained

In the past, I was never one to get out of the office. Over the years, I would work late into the night building my business, but did so in seclusion.

Then in 2011, as I founded my current endeavor, it was obvious to me that this would be a much more multifaceted company. I came to the realization quickly that I would need to do things differently with this one.

After inventing a medical device, I worked hard to determine what I needed to do to move it to market. I knew the product I had invented, a medical infusion device I called RxFusion, was a great product but hardly a company—the market has a need for but it is still a one-off device.

Although I invented RxFusion from a need, I wanted to do something that would have a larger impact and be more than a one-off product. To make this larger impact, it would require a discovery that was much grander.

So, I went on a hunt.

As I started looking for a breakthrough idea around which I could devote my efforts, I talked to many people.

How did I know with whom to talk? I didn't, but I found them through networking.

Networking took me many places

Because of a conversation I had with a friend who was an attorney in Washington DC, I left my home in Arizona and I headed to the nation's capital. I was introduced to the technical transfer people at Johns Hopkins University. I spent some time learning about the great work they were doing and met a lot of people with ideas I might be able to work with.

Not feeling that what they had to offer was what I was looking for, I continued my search and headed north.

I found myself in Rochester, NY—not by mistake, but because the company I owned at the time had an office in the area. In preceding years, I had joined a small local professionals' group, and attended their meetings while visiting the area. I did so whenever my travels and schedule permitted (I also do this in other cities as opportunities arise).

During one of the networking meetings, I was introduced to a person who would become my networking "patient zero" of sorts. This person set off a chain of events for me that resulted in the formation of the company now known as Efferent Labs. This nice lady listened to my story and said she had someone I need to talk with, resulting in the first lesson in networking:

The first lesson in networking—get out of the office

Why did this work for me?

Networking is both an art and a science. The art is in listening to the people you meet and relating to them in a way to gain mutual understanding and a connection.

It is very important that you have an objective when attending any networking event. The objective does not have to be anything more than simply meeting one person.

The science is in the execution: how you identify your objective and take discrete steps to obtain your goal.

The second lesson—have a plan and a goal

It is equally important to have something to give to the contact you meet at an event. This might be as simple as sharing a story, like I did. No matter what—remember this at a networking event: Always have something to give.

I meet a lot of people at networking events. This is what happens when you have a well thought out story, and share it.

When talking to people be genuine; your story will have more meaning and will capture the interest of those you are sharing it with. One of the most important things you can do while at networking events is to ask these like-minded people for referrals. No ask, no results.

Follow-up is as important as attending

Just as important as participating in a networking event is the follow-up. Why spend your time in one of these events if you are not going to follow up? You will never reap any rewards from networking if you do not follow up!

With my "patient zero," I followed up with her the next day. I sent her an email recounting our conversation, and she immediately sent an email introduction to the person she had told me about at the event.

Had I not done a follow-up, the whole cycle would have been a waste of my time. The follow up started the ball rolling for me and led to the next person who in turn introduced me to the next, and ultimately to my goal.

The third lesson—always follow-up

Results are the reward

My quest led me to a lot of people, many of whom I now count as friends.

For me, one person led to the next, and before I knew it I had found what I was looking for.

I was introduced to Spencer Rosero, who would become my co-founder at Efferent Labs. His idea (the insertable biosensor known as CytoComm) had all the earmarks of a company that was worth building. It is a device that can be used in a variety of applications, so it lends itself as the core technology to build a company around.

I knew building this company was not going to be easy, but Spencer and I both believe that the potential benefits to society are large, and the rewards to investors and our team, equally sizable.

I have been introduced to a lot of great people through networking contacts, and they in turn have introduced me to others. Through a string of conversations, I ended up meeting my co-founder and started what is poised to be my most meaningful achievement.

The moral of this story—there is power in networking.

* * *

The Power of Networking

I understand networking can be time consuming and intimidating. In many cases, it also might not give you the results you are hoping for. However, not networking will guarantee zero results.

When I go to networking events, I try to meet as many people as possible. Many times, it is the person standing off to the side, the seemingly shy person who holds the keys to a successful engagement.

You would be surprised how many times I have found this to be a fact. The person might be new to networking, or they do not like to network, maybe he or she is there primarily for the food and drink, but they have a story. Their story, or better yet, their connections might be just what you are looking for to make the event a personal success.

While the people who are crowded with others vying for attention are fully engaged, you might not only make a great connection with that individual standing to the side of the room but a great friend. It is the act of networking that has brought me to where I am today. Over the decades, almost every step in my path has had networking as a key component.

So, get out from behind the screen and start networking.

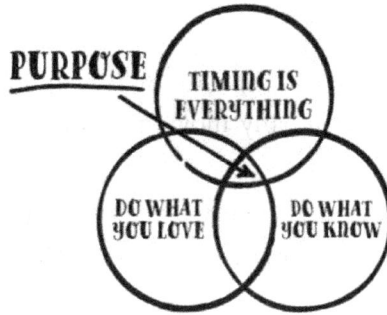

PURPOSE

TIMING IS EVERYTHING

DO WHAT YOU LOVE

DO WHAT YOU KNOW

TEN
The Venn Effect

My Personal Venn

MY PERSONAL VENN STARTED IN THE WATER with my seashell company; however, one could argue it actually started even earlier with the selling of my very first plum.

I still hate plums.

But it was my stay in the Mayo Clinic where I found my purpose. I wanted to really make a marked difference: one so impactful, people around the world would benefit for decades to come. My journey took me to Spencer, who lacked the entrepreneurial experience, but had the technology and, more importantly, the time to make his discovery a success.

We joined forces and in October 2013 officially had a company: Efferent Labs. We had recruited a board and started to design the company. There were stops and starts in the process, but we managed to keep the company moving forward slowly as we found our legs.

We started pitching and then worked our way through a gauntlet to win the 43North competition in October 2014.

Business pitch events are a great way for a young company to gain attention and support. I have written on this topic several times. One of my articles appeared in *Inc.* magazine in 2017:

Inc.—August 2017
Why the Best Way to Fund Your Start-up is Actually the Easiest

Are business competitions a good use of time for a start-up?

A little over three years ago, I asked myself this very question. Are business and pitch competitions a good thing to spend my time on? What I experienced might actually fly against your perceptions.

Here's a breakdown of five common methods of funding a start-up and why competitions are very worth your time:

1. Self-funding or bootstrapping

    You can self-fund or bootstrap your company. Heck, I've done that successfully several times in my business history.

    From my first company until my most recent, I always bootstrapped the effort. It was not easy, but I was beholden only to myself. My thought was that no investors means fewer issues. This can be the case, but it also means no investor support.

2. Applying for grants

    You can apply for grants. This method is usually competitive with very low success rates. Many grants are even harder to apply for and win than a business competition. I have taken the grant route, and it is full of paperwork, qualifications, and waiting.

The success rates are low by any measure, as you are generally competing against professional grant writers. This places your chances at a much lower probability if you don't have a grant writer on staff or under contract.

3. Applying for a loan at the bank

If you have a start-up with little or no real assets, this is a long shot. I've used bank loans to grow companies, mostly in the form of credit lines. Once your company is established and generating revenues, this can be the cheapest way to grow your business, but it requires (in almost all cases) that you place your entire financial future as a bet. If you fail, you are on the line personally, for 100 percent of the borrowed funds. Sure, it sounds like an easy decision—you will never fail! However, I can tell you, you will have sleepless nights when receivables are overdue.

4. "Factoring" receivables

Factoring is the selling of your company's receivables to a "factoring" company. The factoring company then waits for the payment according to your original terms. They commonly charge a discount fee plus interest. This can be very expensive.

Obviously, you will need to have money owed to your company in order to factor. I have historically looked at factoring as a failing company's last lifeline.

However, in recent times I have noted companies using this expensive form of funding as a normal mode of operation. It works for some, but not for me.

5. Competing in business plan competitions

Competitions are fairly common these days, with some offering winners very large sums of cash prizes. A million dollars can be had in at least one regional economic development competition, while others have prizes that are also extremely nice—many in the six-figure range.

Let's talk about competitions

However, not all competitions come with "no strings attached." In fact, many of these high dollar prizes are designed to provide economic development to areas in search of the next Amazon.

In these regional competitions, winners are often required to relocate some, or even all, of their operations to the locality providing the winnings. Fair enough, since those were designed for local economic development.

The odds of a great start-up getting noticed are very high. And, the odds of winning are determined by your direct competition—so your fate is in your hands for the most part.

Bottom line

If you're all-in on your company, you may employ some or all of the options I listed in moving your company forward.

Each route of funding mentioned has its merits and weaknesses. However, don't discount the business competition. There is more than money to gain when being selected as even a semi-finalist. However, as a winner, the intrinsic value is multiplied and can be much greater than the sum of the cash prize.

I personally know many companies that have gone on to win multiple competitions, allowing their company to sustain growth while expanding their footprint, contacts and business knowledge in the effort.

So, if you have a company and are in need of funds, give the business competition a try. You might find out, as I did, that your time was well worth the effort.

* * *

My Venn Purpose

My Venn purpose had taken shape. However, the 43North win came with one hitch: a one-year commitment to living and growing our company in Buffalo—I had to uproot my life in Arizona and head to Buffalo, New York in the middle of winter! So, in late December 2014, we loaded up and moved there.

The move brought with it some interesting by-products, like celebrity status in this former rust-belt community. Almost everywhere I went, people knew who I was and why I was there. This meant a lot of local perks.

But more important than the notoriety was the ability we had to advance the company. The win was like a shot of steroids to Efferent Labs. It gave access to people and companies that otherwise may not have returned my calls.

I was able to meet a lot of people through the 43North

organization, using the win as a conversation starter. I spent time networking to find people and investments to help fuel our company through the difficult stages of development and testing.

It was during this time I determined I would need someone to help me in my current tasks. I advertised for an associate but did not find the person I was looking for.

When I joined 43North, I was supplied a desk in the incubator— an open office shared with about forty other people - a far cry from my offices in the past. I went from the privacy of four walls to a little desk in an open office setting. This was an adjustment for a guy who has operated in a private office for decades. But it had an upside—my future associate was in the same room, and had his eye on joining Efferent since the competition in October 2014.

I wrote a story about this for *Forbes*:

Forbes—July 2016
Hiring on a Shoestring

The Challenge

It's one of the most daunting tasks for a start-up CEO: controlling budget and cash burn. It would be great to say "cash flow" rather than "cash burn." But the reality for me, the CEO of a biotech start-up, is that no money comes into our early-stage company outside of investments.

Every start-up has the same challenge—how to find the right people. I need so many people, but I cannot afford them all. It is crucial to have the right team, but it is equally important to determine a way to determine a way to pay them before I even start searching.

The right person needs to meet specific technical needs, but also have the ability to wear many hats like I do.

The Ideal Hire

To find the right person, you need to look for specific traits:

- Passion for the company mission
- Fit for the role
- Extreme flexibility and adaptability
- The ability to operate outside of their comfort zone

Obviously, the ideal person is more valuable than any start-up can afford. Therefore, you need to get creative to ensure a fair and competitive compensation package.

At Efferent Labs, I started looking for my first full-time employee only a year ago. Prior to that time, I had used only independent contractors. But I needed a person who could seamlessly shift from one role to the work independently and stay the course when things are rough.

"It's a start-up life—one day to the next, even one hour to the next, things change and you must adapt or die."

My budget was way too low for who I needed, so I knew it would be necessary to sweeten the incentive. First, I looked to my personal Rolodex. I know a lot of people in biotech, having spent the last couple decades owning a company in the space.

My first choice was the most qualified and experienced person I knew and respected. But after a lot of discussion about whether he would accept the position, I realized the right person probably didn't need the experience of a mature VP or director. I realized I could grow my own leader!

I connected with local university professors for recommendations. With a 43North win under my belt, my status provided access to local leaders and afforded me the ability to find the right connections to accomplish this task.

I sat down with a local professor who forwarded me a resume, indicating there was no better choice. In many ways, he was right. The individual was knowledgeable, creative, and met almost all of my required check boxes. But there was something that stopped me.

Always listen to that gut feeling. I did and decided to talk to him one more time before making an offer.

I asked him about his opinion of our mission and how he might work with us. The fit had to be right for him. More importantly, he had to be right for the company. The next day, he sent an e-mail thanking me and explained that he was not ready to be in a start-up. My gut feeling was correct!

My Perfect First Hire

My perfect hire needed to have passion for what we are doing, understand start-up culture and commit to our mission. After rebooting the search process, I finally found him.

The question was then about compensation. Like just about all start-ups, we cannot offer the traditional package of a Fortune 500 company—in fact, we are almost diametrically opposite. Stability, security, and set hours are not in our DNA. Luckily, for an ideal hire, the right job is about more than dollars and security. In a start-up, freedom, creativity, stock options, and time off flexibility are just as valuable.

The most important part in start-up employment is to be upfront and honest about risks and rewards. My perfect first hire understood this and was both well-informed and enthusiastic. Our negotiations led to an acceptable offer. I had a gut feeling when I first met with him, and it was correct!

* * *

Time Passes

Over time, we have been able to attract investment from many people. We have also been able to make serious advancements in science and engineering. When I met Spencer, the technology was prototyped and had a very large footprint, way too big for use in people. He had done a lot of upfront testing and worked to make the technology better, but still, the device was very large.

At this point, we have re-engineered the device to a form factor small enough for human use. In fact, our photonics detector is half the size of a pacemaker and is getting smaller all the time. We have been able to look at cells living inside the body and have been able to see pathway activations, all very important in the treatment and diagnosis of disease.

Efferent Labs is poised to make the world-impacting change I have been striving for since my time in the Mayo.

ELEVEN
Intermission

A S A LIFELONG ENTREPRENEUR, I HAVE BEEN through many trials. I started on a high with my first business Aquatic Diving Company. It provided my first lesson as an entrepreneur, not to mention a nice Porsche. Do what you love should be the cornerstone of any entrepreneurial effort.

I followed a great win with a horrible failure, MobiLube: a venture that stripped me of my cash and smashed my pride. But it also taught me a great lesson to add to my personal Venn. Do what you know is a lesson that resonates to this day, many decades later.

My experiences creating a technology company, HT Systems, restored my confidence and allowed for me to recognize there was life after failure. It provided many more lessons and victories with the timing aspect of any venture being a key component. Timing is everything!

My trifecta company, Raland, provided me with great experiences and lessons learned from running a larger company in the service sector. When my world changed with the MS diagnosis, I found myself reflecting on experiences and made a decision that resulted in the inception of my next business venture.

My personal struggle with Multiple Sclerosis directed me toward a different path. It inspired me to invent a medical device, then to create bigger societal changes in healthcare.

I Found my Venn Effect

Every one of these experiences guided me to my purpose—the center of my personal Venn. My purpose, at least at this point in my life, is Efferent Labs. It is the center of my Venn and captures all aspects of the concept needed to create my Venn Effect.

The different lessons and experiences culminated on that day in 2011, when I met Dr. Spencer Rosero. I could apply all the aspects of my experience and life to make a difference so great, that not only could my efforts help millions of people but would also bring me personal fulfillment.

Along my path, I have met many amazing people. Some I included in this book; others who are equally as influential are not included this time, as I choose to keep those stories with me for another day and another purpose. One person who has influenced me was the topic of a story I wrote for *Forbes* in the fall of 2016. This story is about someone who has been in my life for over 30 years. He has also built a Venn purpose in *his* life, and he uses photography as a medium to share it.

Forbes—September 2016
Viewing A Snapshot of History With This Artist and Entrepreneur

Stepping back in time

I approached the door of an old building in the former tobacco mecca of Wilson North Carolina, where a once-booming city is now a quiet town attempting a renaissance, much like so many others around the country.

The area was very quiet and the large red steel doors secure without a doorbell to summon the occupant. I knocked a few times, but quickly realized that it wasn't going to be noticed, so I phoned from my cell to announce my presence.

In a historic building that once housed an indoor car dealership from the early part of the last century, now sits a quiet and even more historic studio. A studio with the walls covered in massive photos: some from nearly 50 years ago, others from as recently as last month. Most are carefully thought out images of the people and places that make the United States very unique, and many others depict a past we might like to forget: the tumultuous time of uncertainty and experimentation, the 1960s.

These are the current studios of Burk Uzzle. Uzzle has been on the front lines of history for over six decades.

From his first assignment, for Jet Magazine taking photos of Dr. Martin Luther King, through today; he has been in and around most any event that has been of political or cultural significance.

His Journey

You might not know him by name, but you know his photos. They are some of the most iconic of the 20th century, spanning from the turbulent era of the 1960s.

He has been documenting history from the jungles of Cambodia and Vietnam Nam to his interesting views of the American experience today.

His photos mark iconic people and important events and are topped with often whimsical and outrageous views of the people and places which are part of his uniquely American experience. These experiences have been cataloged in books and magazines and displayed in just about every major museum.

From the battlefields of Southeast Asia, to the streets of Birmingham during the civil rights marches, he has been in the middle of the action photographing all the emotion and turmoil, fully understanding that he was recording history.

Photojournalist to entrepreneur

Uzzle is more than a photojournalist. He is an artist. But even more, he is an entrepreneur.

Burk started as a 14-year-old photographer with the Raleigh News and Courier but was recognized as a talented photojournalist and was picked up as the youngest photographer ever hired for Life magazine at the age of 23.

He went on to be the president of Magnum photography, leaving when he became troubled that, at the time, only a few in the organization were producing the vast majority of revenues. He said that this was not fair and that he could do better on his own.

From this point on, Burk created his own business and managed every aspect. From the actual creative work to marketing and bookkeeping. He contracts representatives to help him sell his work through large galleries, but he also does some of this himself at his studios in Wilson NC.

"I guess I am an entrepreneur, have been my entire life. The best part is I have been in control of most things when I wasn't being assigned projects."—Burk Uzzle

Famous works

His early photos of Dr. Martin Luther King, Robert Kennedy, and the heart of protests and turmoil are a stark contrast from his photography of Woodstock where he documented the human experience from a different viewpoint. There, his photo of a couple embracing on a muddy hill became the photo that defined the Woodstock generation and was featured as the album cover of the event recordings.

As I viewed his photographs in the museums where they are currently being displayed, I had time to discuss the adventures of this seasoned photographer and businessman in depth. There is a backstory to every photo that is often even more interesting than the picture itself.

One thing I took away from my visit: To live a profitable life as an artist, you must also be a great entrepreneur. Lacking the business skills that Burk clearly has, you are at great risk to end up the proverbial starving artist.

Burk shows the mastery of my top two lessons of entrepreneurship:

Do what you love!

Do what you know!

✳ ✳ ✳

Burk is a special person who has proven through a lifetime of mastery, that my first two principles are the keystone to a successful profession, but more so, to a wonderful life.

100 Percent

At a concert, I accidentally ran into the headline performer, the world-famous jazz pianist Chick Corea, backstage between sets.

Because I have problems when walking due to my past paralysis, in some venues, I am provided an out of the way elevator to ease the journey to my seat in the audience. This was the case when I attended the Chick Corea concert. I was assigned an usher who assisted me to my seat and told me to signal him at the intermission so he could help me if needed.

When the music stopped and the stage emptied for intermission, I let the usher know that I would like to visit the restroom and he obliged. He accompanied me back to the same out-of-the-way elevator I used to get to my seat. But instead of selecting the main level where I had originally entered, he selected the lower level and delivered me to an area usually not accessible to the general public. He said the restrooms in this area were less crowded.

As I exited the elevator, the first person I ran into was the star himself, walking down the hallway.

It was a chance encounter, and I immediately started thinking of something to say other than "Hi!" You don't often have a chance to speak to a world-class performer personally, so I wanted to ask something important.

I quickly complimented him on his completed set, as you might expect, but then I went a step further. I asked him one question:

"If you could do the set over again, what would you change?"

He smiled and said, "Nothing. I left it *all* on the stage."

He then continued down the hallway to finish his break.

This profound statement said more about his professionalism and commitment to his craft than anything I had ever read about him.

Every entrepreneur should also be able to answer this question in the same way.

At the end of the day, when the curtains are drawn on your start-up, you, the founding entrepreneur, must be able to say, "I left it all on the stage." If you can't make this statement with as much confidence as Chick Corea, your efforts were not complete or to the best of your ability.

Every start-up is a challenge from day one. No matter the field or product, the effort required is absolute. You must commit your body, mind, and soul to assure the absolute best outcome for your enterprise. If you put in any less than 100%, even with a successful exit, you didn't get it completely right.

Burk Uzzle demonstrated that entrepreneurism is as much an art as it is a science. It doesn't matter if you're an artist or a scientist, an explorer like Jean-Michel Cousteau, a master corporate innovator like Carl Yankowski, or an entrepreneur hustling your first idea. Your commitment to your craft is the most important thing.

Every successful entrepreneur I have ever known has been driven and focused. Some are true innovators, others great businessmen, but all are committed to their endeavors and always "leave it all on the stage" at the end of the day.

I have spent a lifetime developing my craft, *my* way. I have had major ups and tremendous downs, but I always left it all on the stage.

As I write this, it is only intermission. Right now, I am hip-deep in efforts to move Efferent Labs forward to its full potential to help those with difficult conditions receive better and more accurate medication dosages and treatment.

On my way to this moment, I have encountered all the problems one experiences in a lifetime of business. But my experiences have given me the blessing of wisdom. Wisdom to know when to move and when to stand. Wisdom to use my decades of experience to solve the little problems and accept assistance on the larger ones, and to know the difference between the two.

Experience has also provided me with an appreciation that one cannot necessarily solve every problem. Sometimes you need to adjust your course. But with a good course planned and plotted, you can navigate to the end goal.

I hope the stories of my experiences in this book can help guide you on your course, whether you are a seasoned entrepreneur or a new student to the craft.

It's time for me to get back to work.

AFTERWORD

By —Spencer Z. Rosero, MD

I N THIS BOOK, BILL RADER DETAILS THE life lessons of serial entrepreneurship. I have had the privilege of working with Bill to develop an implantable biosensor using living cells as part of the device to monitor real-time biological activity at the cellular level.

I still remember the day I first met Bill, as an experienced executive who was drawn to upstate New York on business. A serial entrepreneur, Bill had approached the University of Rochester Medical Center looking for nascent health technologies that could be nurtured along to provide real-world changes in medicine. Through a series of coincidences (or not!), the University Office of Technology Transfer set up a meeting between us. At that time, I was refining the concept of cell-embedded implantable biosensors and slowly developing the first large prototype with friends and mentors who had imparted so much of their encouragement and wisdom. During our initial meeting, Bill immediately understood what I was trying to do. At that time, only a few others were able to realize the long-term implications beyond the technology itself.

We were not trying to build an analyte detector, but a living sensor that would reflect what was really going on in the surrounding implanted environment. The sensor cells would do their natural job, doing the job of the "CPU/intel chip," by naturally filtering and processing extracellular signals and initiating algorithms that would result in specific response that we can measure. They would tell us what they are "thinking," and before the individual would even have symptoms.

Needless to say, Bill and I hit it off and we founded Efferent Labs. I'm sure our mutual respect and love for submarines and space travel had something to do with it, (Bill actually worked in a submarine when he was in the US NAVY, while I was just an armchair sub commander reading books and novels on the subject). I first developed the concept for using living cells to serve as the sensor component of an implantable biosensor system after having two patients admitted unexpectedly. One patient was admitted for a life-threatening rhythm and the other with severe heart failure a few days after being seen in an office setting, during which the traditional physiologic data such as blood pressure, heart rate, and blood work was normal, even though both patients "felt something wasn't right."

In addition, both patients had implanted cardiac rhythm devices (also called defibrillators or pacemakers) which provided even more detailed physiologic data during the visit, confirming a normal status. And we still couldn't predict the pending clinical decompensation and hospitalization. I began thinking WOW, so much data and we still cannot predict what happens a few days later. Maybe this traditional data that has served us so well for millennia isn't enough anymore?

The concept of leveraging our own biology to measure cellular processes in real-time came to mind. Why not engineer cell lines to be the sensor component of the hardware? The cells would fluoresce when specific intracellular signals occur BEFORE symptoms and provide a window during which we can intervene. Fluorescence has been used for decades to study biology.

Well, that was easier said than done: I first had to address many questions: How would such a device work? How small can we build it? How can we use it to diagnose and treat disease? Slowly and systematically, and one by one, we have tackled these questions.

As a physician, my long-term goal is to use the sensor to make lives better and healthier. I also believe that advances in this area of technology also provides powerful new research tools to understand better the diseases we are trying to treat and cure.

Efferent Labs was my first foray into entrepreneurship, and it has proven to be a humbling journey balancing the conceptual, academic, and real-life worlds of taking ideas to fruition. While filled with significant ups and downs, periods of fasting while traversing the well-known start-up Valley of Death, the journey has also been and continues to be an unbelievably exciting and challenging adventure. Having Bill as CEO has brought the company to the next level. Personally, he has been a great and sincere friend and a significant source of encouragement with an entrepreneurial endurance worthy of an Olympian in the start-up world.

Spencer Z. Rosero, MD
Chief Medical Officer of Efferent Labs, Inc.

Dr. Rosero is Associate Professor of Medicine and Director, Cardiology Clinical Research at the University of Rochester School of Medicine and Dentistry, where he also serves as Clinical Director at the Center for Medical Technology and Innovation. He is a practicing cardiologist who has developed the CytoComm™ technology through years of work with patients. As a specialist in heart rhythm disorders, Dr. Rosero treats patients using a wide range of therapeutic options, including radiofrequency ablation of abnormal rhythms, implantation of electronic medical devices such as pacemakers, defibrillators (ICD's), and cardiac resynchronization therapy devices. He is an experienced clinical investigator and has actively participated in several large multicenter trials, studying the role of medical devices in treating patients with heart failure and life-threatening arrhythmias. As the site principal investigator for the early evaluation of a novel implantable left atrial pressure monitoring system at the University of Rochester, Dr. Rosero's team was the first in the nation to implant the St. Jude Heart Pod device. His research interests include living cell embedded biosensors, hereditary arrhythmias, and futuristic medical device technologies that support personalization of medical care.

ACKNOWLEDGEMENTS

I would like to acknowledge and thank many people that made this book possible:

Barbara McKenzie
Dan Niles
Greg Gdowski, PhD
James Tanous, Esq.
Cindy Black
Jaymie Collette
Joanna Brougher, Esq., MPH
Jonathan Strimling
Kim Grant
Mary Pat deMey
Patricia Rader
Spencer Rosero, MD
Carl J. Yankowski
The 43North Organization
The New York MedTech Organization

All the others not mentioned above that
have had a significant influence on me over the years.

Illustrations: Anain Roibal